El Salvador

El Salvador

BY MARION MORRISON

Enchantment of the World
Second Series

Children's Press®

A Division of Scholastic Inc.

NEW YORK   TORONTO   LONDON   AUCKLAND   SYDNEY
MEXICO CITY   NEW DELHI   HONG KONG
DANBURY, CONNECTICUT

Frontispiece: Guitars and crafts on display in a shop

Consultant: Louis R. Sadler, Ph.D., Latin American historian and Department Head of History at New Mexico State University

Please note: All statistics are as up-to-date as possible at the time of publication.

Visit Children's Press on the Internet: http://publishing.grolier.com

Book production by Herman Adler Design

Library of Congress Cataloging-in-Publication Data

Morrison, Marion.
    El Salvador / by Marion Morrison
      p. cm. — (Enchantment of the world. Second series)
    Includes bibliographical references and index.
    ISBN 0-516-21118-8
    1. El Salvador—Juvenile literature. [1. El Salvador.] I. Title. II. Series.
F 1483.2 M67 2001
972.84—dc21   00-055570

Acknowledgments

For help in the preparation of this book, I would like to thank the librarians at Canning House and the Royal Geographical Society, London; the Embassy of El Salvador in London; Jason Howe, for some last-minute research in El Salvador; Maria del Carmen Leiva; Nicholas Asheshov; and, perhaps most of all, the people of El Salvador. Their courage and remarkable welcoming nature has been an inspiration.

Contents

Cover photo:
Harvesting flowers
for export

CHAPTER

ONE   Welcome to El Salvador **8**

TWO   Land of Volcanoes and Earthquakes **14**

THREE   Forests, Mangroves, and Wildlife **26**

FOUR   Land of the Jewel **36**

FIVE   A New Democracy **62**

SIX   Rebuilding the Economy **68**

SEVEN   Salvadorans **82**

EIGHT   Changing Faiths **92**

NINE   Arts and Crafts **98**

TEN   Contrasting Lives **110**

Laguna El Jacotal

Timeline **128**

Fast Facts **130**

To Find Out More **134**

Index **136**

A "surprise"

Welcome to El Salvador

8

SHORTLY AFTER DINNER SOME 1,400 YEARS AGO, THE villagers of Joya de Cerén heard the telltale rumble of a deadly earthquake and saw steam exploding from Laguna Caldera Volcano. The village was not far from San Salvador, now the capital of El Salvador. All the people could do was run for their lives, leaving all their possessions behind. In a short time, volcanic rocks, lava, and ash completely covered Joya de Cerén. Archaeologists believe that everyone escaped. So far, no bodies have been found.

The village was discovered in 1976 when a worker accidentally dug into the site with a bulldozer. It was covered in up to 20 feet (6 meters) of ash. This exciting scientific find revealed a village, probably built by Mayan people. The site gives us a fascinating look at how these ancient tribes lived.

Opposite: **People in San Salvador build their homes close to the volcano.**

Ruins of the Mayan village at Joya de Cerén

Among the earthen structures excavated so far are houses, storage areas, and rooms that probably had a religious function. One of those is known as the *Casa del Brujo* (House of the Shaman). One building in a public area contained some artifacts and a turtle-shell drum, suggesting a music or dancing room. Another building housed a sort of Mayan sauna, probably also for communal use. The many artifacts included painted ceramics and utensils for cooking and storage, jars full of petrified beans, stone implements, the skull and bones of a deer, and a pot containing the head of a caiman—a kind of crocodile.

Gardens with neat rows of corn have also been discovered, along with evidence of other crops including beans, agave, cacao, peppers, guava, cotton, and tobacco. Clearly, the villagers had a variety of food, and their society seems to have been stable and well organized.

Much of El Salvador's more recent history has been turbulent, however. In the 1500s, the land was conquered by Spanish explorers. It was a Spanish colony for about 300 years. Unlike many other places in Latin America, El Salvador had neither gold nor silver. Instead, it had good farmland, made fertile by the same volcanic eruptions that from time to time have devastated the land.

El Salvador joined the Central American Federation in 1823, and became an independent republic in 1841 after the federation collapsed in 1839. By that time, the pattern of society was set. Most land was owned by a few wealthy families. Those families, supported by the army, have controlled the economy and the people of El Salvador ever since. Many people

Fertile farmland in Los Naranjos

Geopolitical map of
El Salvador

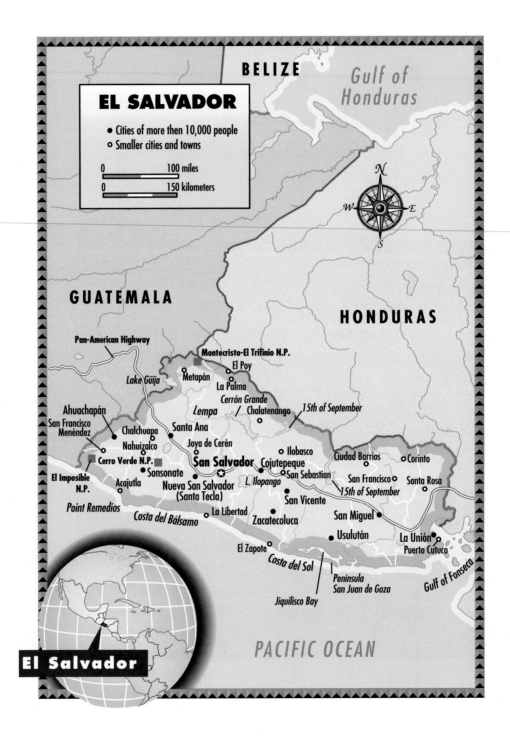

EL SALVADOR

- Cities of more then 10,000 people
- Smaller cities and towns

0   100 miles

0   150 kilometers

BELIZE

Gulf of
Honduras

N
W   E
S

GUATEMALA

HONDURAS

Pan-American Highway

Montecristo-El Trifinio N.P.
El Poy
Metapán
La Palma
Lake Güija
Cerrón Grande
Lempa   Chalatenango
15th of September

Ahuachapán
San Francisco
Menéndez
Chalchuapa   Santa Ana
Nahuizalco   Joya de Cerén
Cerro Verde N.P.
El Imposible
N.P.   Sonsonate
Acajutla
Nueva San Salvador
(Santa Tecla)
Point Remedios
Costa del Bálsamo   La Libertad

San Salvador
Cojutepeque
Ilobasco
San Sebastian
L. Ilopango
Ciudad Barrios   Corinto
San Francisco   Santa Rosa
15th of September
San Vicente
San Miguel
Zacatecoluca
Usulután
La Unión
El Zapote   Puerto Cútuco
Costa del Sol
Peninsula
San Juan de Goza
Jiquilisco Bay
Gulf of Fonseca

El Salvador

PACIFIC OCEAN

who have spoken out against this injustice have been silenced, in particular Archbishop Oscar Romero, who was assassinated in 1980.

Earthquakes have hit the country many times. San Salvador has been destroyed twice and badly damaged on several occasions. Many people have lost their lives. El Salvador also suffers many volcanic eruptions, and San Miguel, the largest city in eastern El Salvador, has been particularly badly hit.

The worst recent disaster to strike this troubled land was a civil war that raged from 1980 to1992, resulting in the deaths of 75,000 people. The war was essentially a conflict between the wealthy ruling families supported by the army, and left-wing guerrillas. Time will tell us if peace can bring the social and economic changes El Salvador so desperately needs.

A memorial to victims of the civil war

Land of Volcanoes and Earthquakes

14

EL SALVADOR IS THE SMALLEST AND THE MOST DENSELY populated country in Latin America. It is slightly smaller than Massachusetts, measuring only 163 miles (262 kilometers) at its widest point. A bus journey across the country takes only a few hours. To the south, El Salvador faces the Pacific Ocean with a coastline of 191 miles (307 km). Its northern and eastern borders touch the Republic of Honduras, and it borders Guatemala on the west.

In spite of its small size and large population, El Salvador is a beautiful country. Behind the coastline, narrow plains are backed by lofty mountains. In the south, these ranges are volcanic and reach an average height of 4,000 feet (1,219 m). The northern mountain ranges are higher. Along the border with Honduras, Cerro El Pital is the country's highest mountain at 8,957 feet (2,730 m). Running from the west to the southeast, a central plain occupies about one-fourth of the total area and contains the valley of the Río Lempa, El Salvador's largest and only navigable river.

The Lempa is the largest river.

El Salvador's Geographical Features

Area: 8,124 square miles (21,040 sq km)

Highest Elevation: Cerro El Pital, 8,957 feet (2,730 m) above sea level

Lowest Elevation: Sea level along the Pacific Ocean

Longest River: Río Lempa, 200 miles (322 km) long; 150 miles (241 km) of the Lempa flows through El Salvador

Largest Lake: Lake Ilopango, 25 square miles (65 sq km)

Volcanoes: El Salvador has a range of twenty volcanic mountains; the highest is Santa Ana, 7,812 feet (2,381 m) above sea level

Earthquakes: Recent earthquakes took place in 2001, causing the deaths of more than 1,000 people

Coastline: 191 miles (307 km) along the Pacific Ocean

Highest Annual Precipitation: 85 inches (216 centimeters) along the coast

Lowest Annual Precipitation: less than 60 inches (152 cm) in the northwest

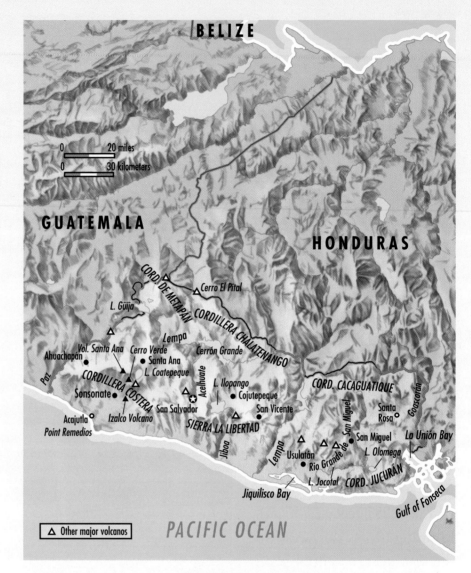

Highest Average Temperature: 94°F (34°C), in San Salvador in March

Lowest Average Temperature: 60°F (16°C), in San Salvador in January

Greatest Distance North to South: 88 miles (142 km)

Greatest Distance East to West: 163 miles (262 km)

Origins

The land that is now El Salvador was created by the enormous movements of the Earth's tectonic plates. These movements began in the late Paleozoic era, which ended 225 million years ago. Scientists believe that the world's landmass was once a single huge continent, called Pangaea. In the late Paleozoic era, Pangaea began to break into two parts—Laurasia, in the north, and Gondwanaland, in the south. As the movement continued, it eventually led to the two American continents and the connecting region known today as Central America.

The South American continent began to separate from Gondwanaland about 130 million years ago. It became an island, where animal life evolved in isolation. About 20 million years ago, smaller islands began to appear in the sea separating the two American continents. These islands often were volcanic. They made contact possible between North America and South America. By 3 million to 4 million years ago, an unbroken land connection had replaced the separate islands. We know this area as Central America. Ever since its appearance, it has continued to develop through weathering and geological upheaval.

Volcanoes and Earthquakes

Life for the Salvadoran people has often been touched by forces beneath the ground. Salvadorans know their country as a "land of volcanoes and earthquakes." The huge eruption of Volcano Ilopango around A.D. 250 covered much of the country with ash. Thousands of Maya people died, and many survivors fled

The Pacific Ring of Fire

○ Volcanoes, Ring of Fire
— Tectonic Plates

View of Lake Ilopango

to other centers of civilization. Today, the remains of these civilizations are in Guatemala and Belize.

The Ilopango eruption left extensive ash beds as well as Lake Ilopango—a favorite weekend spot for many Salvadorans today. Geologically, it is known as a *caldera* lake because of the way it was formed. Instead of coming from a single enormous explosion, a section of land probably subsided, leaving steep sides like the rim of an ancient volcano. Over time, these

Lighthouse of the Pacific

Izalco Volcano is called the "Lighthouse of the Pacific" because its frequent, fiery eruptions were seen far out at sea. Izalco was once the most active volcano in El Salvador and one of the most active in all the Americas. It is 6,396 feet (1,950 m) high.

Izalco began life in 1770 as a small hole in the ground. Since then, it has erupted at least fifty-one times, emitting streams of lava and ash that have built

a near-perfect cone rising above the surrounding countryside. The lower parts of its slopes are now covered with coffee plantations, and a visitor trail leads to the summit crater.

People can watch the activity from a small hotel on nearby Cerro Verde, part of an ancient volcano that lies within a national park. Izalco's last, minor eruption occurred in 1966. Since then, it has been quiet.

sides weathered and the caldera filled with water. The sides are craggy and covered with vegetation that creates privacy for private land and homes. In 1879–1880, a small volcano named *Las Islas Quemadas* (The Burnt Islands) rose above the surface of the lake.

More recently, in October 1986, a major earthquake struck the San Salvador area. It left 1,500 people dead and almost 500,000 homeless. The earthquake also damaged many public buildings in the capital, some of which collapsed. Then, in January and February 2001, more than 1,000 people died in two more earthquakes. These were not the first disasters to strike central El Salvador. In 1756 and again in 1854, San Salvador was largely destroyed. In 1917, another earthquake hit the area, and the volcano Boqueron, within the old San Salvador volcano next to the capital. A lake that had formed in the crater boiled and totally evaporated within three weeks.

Many of El Salvador's larger towns and villages are near volcanoes because the soil surrounding them is especially fertile. Altogether, more than twenty volcanoes line the southern mountains. They are clustered into five groups as they spread across the country. The highest volcano is Santa Ana, at 7,812 feet (2,381m).

Mountain Ranges

El Salvador is a land of broad vistas from one mountain range to another across carefully tended farmland. Volcanoes dominate in the south, while the northern mountains are made up of several *cordilleras* (ranges). The names of the cordilleras come from the original Indian languages. The Cordillera de Metapán lies along the northern border where the Río Lempa enters the country. In the east, the cordilleras of Nahuacaterique and Cacaguatique surround the department of Morazán.

Department of Morazán

El Salvador's isolated and rugged department of Morazán is named for Francisco Morazán (right), a visionary leader and general from neighboring Honduras. Morazán was born in 1792. His modest family's roots were in the European island of Corsica. Young Francisco began working in a store and ended up as a famous general and president of Costa Rica. He fought hard to achieve his vision—a united, federal Central America.

Today, Morazán remains isolated, with a population of less than 200,000. The main river is the Río Grande de San Miguel, which flows southward between mountains dominated by fields of *henequen* (a fiber used to make rope, bags, and hammocks) and pine forests. The mountains hold gold and silver, and their highest point, on the western side of the department, is Cerro Cacaguatique, 5,456 feet (1,663 m). Not far from the small settlement of Corinto in the Cordillera Nahuacaterique are the caves of Espíritu Santo and *Cabeza de Duende* (Head of the Goblin). Paintings from pre-Columbian times decorate the walls of these caves.

El Salvador's rocky Pacific coastline

The Pacific Coast

While mountain ranges, volcanoes, and lush valleys dominate the interior, the Pacific coast and its low-lying hinterland account for about one-tenth of El Salvador's land. The hot and humid coast stretches from the Río Paz in the west to the Gulf of Fonseca in the east. The coastline is varied, with

Looking at El Salvador's Cities

Santa Ana (right) is El Salvador's second-largest city. Located in a mountain basin in the northwest, it stands at an altitude of 2,182 feet (665 m). Known as Santa Ana since 1708, the city is an important commercial and industrial center. Coffee, grown on nearby hills, is processed there in one of the world's largest coffee mills. Other important products made in Santa Ana include cigars, leather goods, cotton textiles, and furniture. A branch of the University of El Salvador makes Santa Ana an educational center. Visitors enjoy touring historic landmarks such as the Spanish Gothic cathedral built in the early 1900s and El Calvario, a colonial church. Many stay at summer resorts at nearby Lake Coatepeque. Ruins of the Indian city of Chalchuapa are 9 miles (14 km) west of Santa Ana. Santa Ana Volcano, the country's tallest, is near the city.

San Miguel, the country's third-largest city, lies in the east along the Río Grande de San Miguel. San Miguel Volcano rises above the city. Residents endure a sticky heat most of the year, with temperatures averaging 77° Fahrenheit (25°C) in January and 83°F (28°C) in July. Spanish settlers founded the city in 1530. Crops grown in the region include coffee, cotton, sugarcane, and grain. San Miguel's industries, based on these crops, include the production of cotton textiles, rope, and leather goods. Goods are shipped to and from San Miguel by trucks and railways. San Miguel also has a branch of the University of El Salvador. Visitors can tour the city's eighteenth-century cathedral, view an art show at the Antigua Teatro Nacional, or venture out to Ruinas de Quelepa, the ruins of an ancient Indian town.

Nueva San Salvador (also called Santa Tecla), the country's fourth-largest city, is a few miles west of San Salvador. Surrounded by mountains, the city is at the base of San Salvador Volcano. Nueva San Salvador was built after an earthquake greatly damaged San Salvador in 1854. This new city was El Salvador's capital until 1859, when the capital was moved back to San Salvador. Today, Nueva San Salvador is a middle-class suburb of San Salvador. Although the Pan American Highway divides the city in two, Nueva San Salvador is a quiet town with two pretty parks. A cultural museum is located in Parque San Martín.

Ahuachapán, the country's fifth-largest city, is near the Guatemalan border in western El Salvador. It lies at an altitude of 2,470 feet (753 m) along the Río Molino at the base of La Lagunita Volcano. Founded by Indians in the A.D. 400s, the town survived conquests by the Pipil in the 1400s and the Spanish in the 1500s. Today, Ahuachapán is an important coffee manufacturing and distribution center. Hot mineral springs draw many visitors, and since 1975, heat from the springs has also provided power for a geothermal power plant.

palm-fringed sandy beaches, rocky cliffs, mangrove swamps, and shallow bays. One of the largest is Jiquilisco Bay, southeast of San Salvador. Many small rivers drain into the bay, which is fringed by mangroves and has numerous islands.

A road just inland from the sea connects the major towns and villages, which are now centers of agricultural production. Areas almost directly south of the capital are known as the Costa del Sol and the Costa del Bálsamo. The Costa del Bálsamo is named for the old trade in natural balsam, used in medicines. Here, the mountains rise abruptly from the sea, and numerous deep valleys carry streams whose sources are on the slopes of San Salvador Volcano. The palm-fringed beaches have black volcanic sand, and the coast is popular with weekend tourists who enjoy swimming and surfing.

Rivers and Lakes

El Salvador has more than 300 rivers, but their courses are short. The longest river is the Lempa, which rises in Guatemala and crosses a small part of Honduras before entering El Salvador near the northern border town of El Poy. The total length of the Río Lempa is approximately 200 miles (322 km), and about three-quarters of its waters flow through El Salvador.

The Lempa, which is navigable for part of its course, is economically important. Since the 1960s, it has been used to produce hydroelectric power. Dams create two lakes—the Cerrón Grande, surrounded by stony slopes, and the Fifteenth of September, which is at a lower altitude. The Lempa finally enters the Pacific Ocean through a long estuary southeast of San Salvador, the Bocana Río Lempa.

Other notable rivers are the Grande de San Miguel and the Goascarán. These rivers drain eastern El Salvador. The Grande de San Miguel enters the Pacific in another low-lying estuary, the Bocana La Chepona. The Goascarán, which rises in neighboring Honduras, forms the border for much of its length. It reaches the ocean through the Bahía de La Unión (Union Bay) in the Gulf of Fonseca.

In addition to lakes created by dams, El Salvador has several natural lagoons. Ilopango is the largest. Lago de Coatepeque, west of San Salvador, fills another ancient crater at an altitude of 2,365 feet (721 m).

Climate

El Salvador's climate is tropical, with little change of temperature other than that due to altitude. In San Salvador, the average temperature is around 74° Fahrenheit (23°C), while on the coast, it is 83°F (28°C). In the high northern mountains, the average is about 64°F (18°C), with near-freezing temperatures recorded occasionally. Rain, heavy from May to October, averages almost 71 inches (180 cm). The rest of the year is dry, leaving some parts of the country extremely arid and in danger of becoming desert. One estimate suggests that 50 percent of the cleared land in El Salvador is severely eroded or degraded.

Forests, Mangroves, and Wildlife

A s THE ANCIENT "LAND BRIDGE" BETWEEN TWO CONtinents, Central America had an enormous variety of animal life. Species arrived there from the isolated south and from the north. The range of altitude, climate, freshwater, and effects of the ocean influenced the plant life. Tropical forests were extensive. Today, however, the situation has changed. According to the International Union for the Conservation of Nature, El Salvador has the lowest biological diversity in the region and the most altered landscape in Central America.

The reasons are not hard to find. Overpopulation heads the list, followed by intensive agriculture. One estimate from the

Opposite: **A colibri perched in Montecristo National Park.**

The National Flower and Tree

El Salvador's national flower is the *izote* (right), from the yucca plant. Yuccas, which are related to lilies, are typical plants of the southern United States, Mexico, and Central America. The *izote* is large and treelike. Its numerous flowers are ivory-white or cream-colored.

The national tree is the *maquilishuat,* or pink poui, tree. It produces pink blossoms from January to April and grows up to 60 feet (18.3 m) tall. This tree belongs to the Bignonia family, named after a seventeenth-century French naturalist. In Spanish, *maquilishuat* wood is often known as *roble* (oak). It is used for fine furniture and home interiors.

The National Bird

El Salvador's national bird is a motmot known as the *Torogoz*—a small bird with two long tail feathers hanging below the body. These birds generally inhabit bushes but are sometimes seen in gardens. Bird-watchers see an almost rhythmical flicking of the tail from one side to the other.

United Nations (UN) Food and Agricultural Organization suggests that only 6 percent of the original forest survives. Even the mangrove forests in the estuaries are being cut for fuel and to produce tannin for industry. Fortunately, measures are now being taken to protect the remaining wildlife.

High in the northwestern corner of El Salvador, close to the junction with Honduras and Guatemala, is Montecristo National Park. The park, bathed in almost perpetual clouds, holds a fine example of a mountain rain forest. Montecristo is part of the three-country El Trifinio International Biosphere Reserve centered on the mountain Cerro Montecristo in the Cordillera Metapán Alotepque.

A mangrove forest

Montecristo National Park

Rainfall in Montecristo National Park reaches almost 79 inches (200 cm) a year. Trees here are covered with countless *epiphytes*, or air plants. These bromeliads, orchids, mosses, and lichens thrive in the damp rain forest. They form a very specialized ecosystem high in the trees—a world of insects, flowers, and tropical birds. Among the bird species are hummingbirds, toucans, quetzals, and striped owls. Spider monkeys and opossums are among the tree-dwelling mammals. In some places, the vegetation and the trees—including Guatemalan firs and giant ferns—are so dense that sunlight does not reach the ground level. This lower level of rain-soaked and rotting vegetation is home to a few species of large mammals. Deer, foxes, and the occasional jaguar have been reported.

An important part of Salvadoran conservation is an organization known as SalvaNatura. Founded in 1989, the group is dedicated to the management and study of the nation's remaining natural environment and wildlife.

The flagship project of SalvaNatura is *Bosque El Imposible* (The Impossible Forest) National Park, in the extreme southwest of the country. *El Imposible* is one of Central America's few remaining rain forests. The name comes from a place known as the "Impossible Pass" on a mule trail between the coffee lands of Ahuachapán and the coast. El Imposible covers more than 12,000 acres (5,000 hectares) in the Cordillera de Apaneca-Ilamatepec near the town of San Francisco Menéndez. The altitude in the park ranges from 984 feet (300 m) to 4,593 feet (1,400 m), with some exceptionally steep forested hillsides.

SalvaNatura has been managing the park since 1990. The organization says that the park holds more than 400 species of trees and more than 260 species of birds, including curassows, king vultures, hummingbirds, and migrants. The many insects include more than 300 species of butterflies. Among the mammals are Tamandua anteaters (known as *osos hormigueros* or ant bears), and rare pumas called cougars or mountain lions. A river

A Tamandua anteater

called the *Mixtepe* gets its name from an old Indian word meaning "the hill of the pumas." More than eight rivers flow to the Pacific Ocean from El Imposible. The rivers play an important part in the delicately balanced mangrove forest ecosystem of the Barra de Santiago. Healthy mangroves need a specific balance of saltwater and freshwater.

SalvaNatura also protects another natural area known as Los Volcanes National Park. The park consists of three volcanoes—Cerro Verde, Santa Ana, and Izalco.

Mangroves and Wetlands

Tropical mangrove forests line shallow coastal lagoons at the mouths of rivers. They are usually rich in wildlife. At the lowest level, the water and mud surrounding the mangrove roots are home to small crabs, insects, and fish. When the tide is out, migratory wading birds feed at the shoreline. The trees provide roosting places for colonies of egrets, while herons and ospreys watch for prey from the branches.

An egret catches food.

In El Salvador, water pollution, shrimp farming, and tree cutting have upset the ecosystem of many mangrove forests. Luckily, the Barra de Santiago is relatively untouched. Here, in the waters of the estuary, the curious gar fish still exists. Gars are a relic of the Eocene Period, 58 to 37 million years ago. They are heavily armored with thick, diamond-shaped scales. The *machorra* of El Salvador, which weigh up to 40 pounds (18 kilograms), have a long mouth full of teeth. They are predators that feed on large quantities of smaller fish. Often they bask near the surface, where they breathe air.

Wetlands—areas of shallow lakes, swamps, or marshes—are endangered in El Salvador, as they are all over the world. The pressure of people living in the area constantly threatens tiny Laguna El Jocotal, in the floodplain valley of the Río Grande de San Miguel within 11 miles (18 km) of the coast. This lagoon is seldom more than 3.3 feet (1 m) deep except during the rainy season. It is home to many waterbirds and also provides a resting place for migratory birds, such as the blue-winged teal, on their way north and south across the

The Tree Duck Saga

The tree ducks, or whistling ducks, of Laguna El Jocotal are known locally as *pichiches*. For years, they have been an important source of protein for people living along the lagoon. But as the number of people increased, so did their demand for food.

In 1976, some protection was given to the lagoon by the nation's Parks Service when a survey revealed that only 500 ducks remained. Trees and other nesting cover had been destroyed. The answer turned out to be nesting boxes! Over the next five years, dozens of nesting boxes were placed around the lake, and the ducks soon adapted to them. Now the ducks are plentiful once more, and their eggs are harvested by a local cooperative.

Americas. More than 130 species of aquatic birds have been sighted, but the lagoon is best known for its resident population of tree ducks, or whistling ducks.

Laguna El Jocotal is very shallow in the dry seaon.

Gulf of Fonseca

Another troubled wetland area is the Gulf of Fonseca. Here too, problems are now being recognized, but not yet solved. This shallow inlet of the sea is shared by El Salvador, Honduras, and Nicaragua. Its waters cover 778 square miles (2,015 sq km), and it has a coastline of more than 248 miles (400 km). Like other inlets with restricted access to the ocean, the gulf is easily polluted. Most people living along its shores have no sewage systems and no way to dispose of garbage. Agricultural chemicals used on farms drain off into the gulf, and many mangrove forests have been cut down for firewood.

The Gulf of Fonseca is shared by three nations.

Mangrove forests have been cut to provide firewood.

These and other problems introduced by human activity have affected the aquatic wildlife, especially the larvae of shrimps. Shellfish have been affected too, and the future of life in the gulf is seriously endangered. These problems affect the local people and their livelihood.

The Future

The balance between people and the environment in El Salvador is one of the most delicate in the Western Hemisphere. The directors of SalvaNatura are promoting programs for education and simple waste disposal in and around El Imposible.

One beneficial aspect of El Salvador's long civil war was a reduction in pesticide use by some coastal farms as cotton production declined. A downside of peace is that more land has been cleared for cultivation. It will always be difficult to strike the right balance as the population increases. The best chance for the remaining wildlife lies in the success of the national parks and reserves.

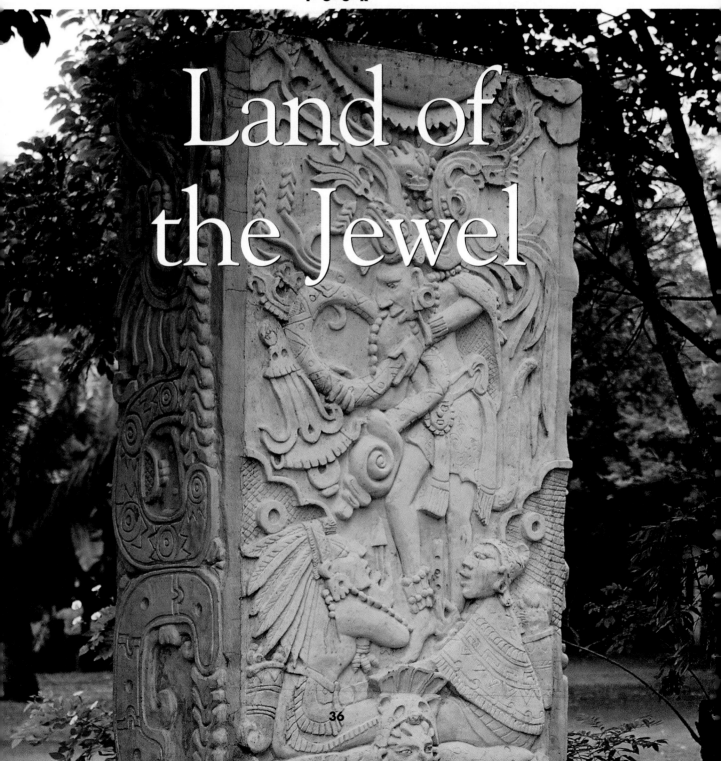

Land of the Jewel

THE EARLIEST CIVILIZED PEOPLES TO SETTLE IN THE LAND that is now El Salvador included the Maya, the Lenca, and the Pipil. All were descendants of primitive humans who made their way from Asia to the Americas across the frozen Bering Strait at the end of the last Ice Age. When these people changed from hunting and gathering to growing crops—sometime between 4000 and 1000 B.C.—the first cultures began to emerge.

The Maya probably arrived in what is now El Salvador around 1200 B.C. They originated in Mexico, where they were influenced by the first highly developed civilization, the Olmec, who lived on Mexico's Gulf coast. The Maya spread south, where their main center was in Guatemala.

A Mayan settlement in San Andres

Over the next 700 years, the Maya created important settlements in western and central El Salvador, including Chalchuapa (near what is now Santa Ana) and Tazumal. Their economy was based on farming, and they grew a variety of crops, especially maize, as well as beans and squash. Some of the fruits and vegetables were unknown in Europe, such as

A Mayan ceramic bowl

tomatoes, peppers, and pineapples. They also traded ceramics and obsidian—a hard, black, semiprecious volcanic glass used to make tools and ornaments.

The Mayan civilization reached its peak between A.D. 300 and 900, a period known as Classic Maya. By that time, the Maya had acquired a highly sophisticated knowledge of the arts of weaving, sculpture, ceramics, and painting. They had developed a form of hieroglyphic writing that experts are still unraveling, and their advanced knowledge of mathematics and astronomy allowed them to create an accurate calendar to regulate their agricultural year. Surprisingly, they did not use the wheel for any practical purpose—such as transport or agriculture—even though they used wheels on children's toys.

Toward the end of the tenth century, the Classic Maya civilization collapsed. No one is sure why. Sometime after that, groups of Nahuatl-speaking people associated with the Aztecs of Mexico migrated south. They settled along the Pacific coast of Guatemala and El Salvador, where they became known as the Pipil. They called their land *Cuscatlán*, meaning "Land of the Jewel."

Pipil society was well organized, with a chief, priests, administrators, and warriors. They also had a large number of artisans, including potters, carpenters, weavers, and stone-masons. Religion was important, and their principal gods were the sun and rain, which were vital to farmers. Maize was the Pipil's main crop, but they also grew cacao (for chocolate), which they traded widely in the region, and tobacco. Of the several towns the Pipil created, Ahuachapan and Sonsonate are still important centers.

A Visit to Tazumal

Tazumal is El Salvador's main archaeological site. It lies within the town of Chalchuapa, a short bus ride from Santa Ana. The Tazumal site has been occupied since 5000 B.C.

The central structure, which is also the largest structure, is a fourteen-step pyramid that dates back to the Maya. The pyramid probably was built in stages, over perhaps 750 years. Originally, a number of other temples and a ball court were attached to it. Tombs on the northern edge of the site have revealed jewelry and other artifacts that suggest trading was taking place with peoples as far away as Mexico and Panama.

After the fall of the Maya, the Pipil occupied the site and expanded it. Tazumal was finally abandoned around A.D. 1200.

In 1524, Hernan Cortés, conqueror of Mexico, sent Spanish troops led by Pedro de Alvarado to subdue the peoples of Guatemala and El Salvador. In both regions, Alvarado faced more opposition than he had expected. Entering western El Salvador from Guatemala in June 1524, he found the Pipil prospering in fertile valleys. Their military forces were well organized. Life centered mainly on two city states—Cuscatlán, where San Salvador is today; and Tecpa Izalco, in the Sonsonate area. With some 250 Spanish troops and a large force of Indian warriors from central Mexico, Alvarado initially defeated the Pipil and advanced toward Cuscatlán. He found the city deserted because the Pipil army had fled into the mountains.

Pedro de Alvarado

Alvarado went back to Guatemala and the next year returned to El Salvador, where he founded the town of San Salvador. Again, the Pipil fought fiercely. This time, they forced the Spaniards to withdraw. It was not until 1528, after several more Spanish expeditions, that San Salvador was firmly established and the region finally conquered. Indian uprisings by the Lenca and others delayed the conquest of the land east of the Río Lempa for several years.

The colony of El Salvador was divided into two provinces. San Salvador covered about three-fourths of the country to the east. In the west, the province of Sonsonate was based on the Pipil territory of Izalco.

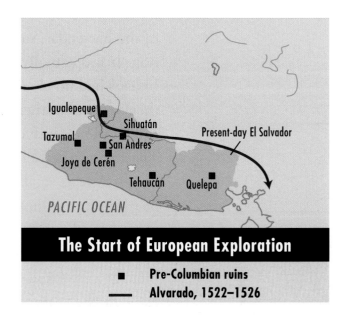

The Spaniards were disappointed that their new colony did not have the gold and minerals they wanted. Its most valuable asset was fertile land, so the Spaniards lost no time in dividing it up among themselves. They introduced and raised cattle, but cacao was the most important crop during the 1500s. It grew best on the Pacific coast and was used to make chocolate for the fashionable salons of Europe.

By the end of the sixteenth century, competition from other colonies and a change in fashion led to a reversal of fortune. El Salvador's economy was in decline for most of the seventeenth century. But by the mid-eighteenth century, fortunes were again restored by the trade in indigo, a blue dye used to color textiles. Indigo became the main export.

Only a handful of Spanish families known as *Los catorce grandes* (the Fourteen Families) enjoyed wealth and prosperity, however. These families had divided the land into enormous estates, or haciendas. Most of the population worked as virtual slaves on these haciendas. The Spaniards introduced the *encomienda* system under which the native workers were tied to the haciendas, supposedly in return for a Christian education. It was actually a form of slavery. In effect, it meant the Indians had no chance of ever being free and could not work their way out of their miserable conditions.

But the greatest danger the Indians faced was from disease. The Spanish settlers unknowingly introduced infectious illnesses such as smallpox and influenza to which the Indians had little or no immunity. It is estimated that by the end of the sixteenth century, about half the native population had died. Forced to look elsewhere for workers, the Spanish then brought in black slaves from Africa. The practice was stopped early in the seventeenth century, when the African slaves showed signs of rebellion.

During the eighteenth century, colonial society became clearly defined. There were two small upper classes. A tiny, Spanish-born elite supported by the Catholic Church held power and governed the colony, while much of the wealth from trading and most of the haciendas belonged to Creoles— Spaniards born in the colony. Most of the people were Indians or mestizos born of mixed Indian and Spanish parents.

Independence

Mexico and the Central American colonies wanted independence from Spain for many of the same reasons South American countries did. The colonies were required to pay taxes to the Spanish Crown, and trading restrictions heavily favored Spain. In Central America, there was also a sharp decline in indigo exports in the first decade of the nineteenth

José Matías Delgado

The first call for independence for the province of San Salvador came in 1811, when a priest named José Matías Delgado rang the bells of the Church of La Merced. Born in 1767 of a Panamanian father and Guatemalan mother, Delgado studied theology and law in Guatemala. From 1821 to 1823, he was the political chief of San Salvador, and in 1824, he published the first Salvadoran newspaper.

century. The colonists saw their opportunity when the Spanish king was expelled from his throne by Joseph Bonaparte, brother of Emperor Napoléon Bonaparte of France. Uprisings in San Salvador led by José Matías Delgado and his nephew Manuel José Arce in 1811 and in 1814 were put down, however.

Mexico gained its independence in 1821, and the Mexican general Agustín de Iturbide, who had been born in Spain, proposed the creation of a Mexican empire to include the Central American territories. Guatemala agreed, but the Salvadorans did not, and war broke out between the two. In 1822, the Salvadoran Congress proposed that the province be annexed to the United States, but the scheme was abandoned the following year when the Mexican empire collapsed and Iturbide was deposed.

In 1823, the United Provinces of Central America was created, with Manuel José Arce as its first president. It lasted until 1838, when it was torn apart by ideological differences between Conservatives, who represented the old order of church,

Manuel José Arce

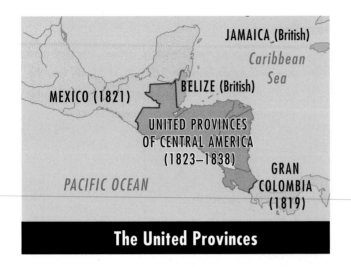

The United Provinces

army, and wealthy landowners, and Liberals, who were antichurch, wanted land and judicial reform and encouraged immigration. By 1839, El Salvador was the only territory left in the federation.

Although Arce was a Liberal, he allied with the Conservatives. This led to a bloody war from 1826 to 1829, won by the Liberals led by Honduran general Francisco Morazán. The people of San Salvador supported Morazán, and he repaid their support when he became president of the federation by making San Salvador the capital of the United Provinces.

Morazán continued as president after an election in 1834, when the winning candidate died before taking office. The deep division between the Liberals and Conservatives continued, leading to Morazan's downfall in 1840. By that time, Nicaragua, Honduras, and Costa Rica had already left the federation. In 1841, the Republic of El Salvador was founded.

The Aquino Rebellion

A serious, month-long uprising in 1833 was led by Anastasio Aquino, an Indian working on an indigo plantation. Aquino's brother had been imprisoned and apparently forced into labor by a hacienda owner. The protest involved the wider issue of land ownership. The government had decreed that all land not in use should pass into private ownership—that is, to the wealthy landowners. This deprived the ordinary people of any chance to acquire land of their own. Thousands of Indians and mestizos joined the so-called Army of Liberation, demanding "land for those who work it." They had some military success against the government and a chance to take over San Salvador. But government troops got the upper hand, and Aquino was captured and executed.

A Coffee Republic

The situation in El Salvador from 1841 to 1876 was even worse than it had been before independence. Presidents came and went, bringing innumerable changes in government. Only after 1860 did any leader last longer than a few months. The rivalry between Conservatives and Liberals was intense, and El Salvador was constantly in conflict with its neighbors, in particular with dictator Rafael Carrera, who ruled Guatemala from 1839 until his death in 1865.

During the 1860s, coffee became an important commercial crop. It had been grown in El Salvador since the 1840s, and when indigo dye ceased to be profitable following the introduction of artificial dyes, many landowners turned to coffee production. The government encouraged the new industry with a policy that hurt most Salvadorans.

In 1882, Liberal president Rafael Zaldivar (1876–1885) passed laws to privatize communal lands. These were the only lands on which Indian communities and peasant families could grow crops for their own use. But the government took over the lands and offered them to anyone prepared to grow coffee. The people protested, but their demonstrations were vigorously put down by a newly created mounted police force.

At the end of the nineteenth century, El Salvador was still controlled by a tiny but extremely powerful elite made up of landowners—many of them coffee growers—and some immigrant planters from Europe. Three-quarters of all the land was owned by just 2 percent of the population. The powerful and wealthy people invested in other trades and products too.

Politically, they controlled the government and made sure the president supported them. They also had the support of the powerful Catholic Church.

In the early years of the twentieth century, profits from the coffee industry contributed to improvements in transport—particularly railways—and education, but these improvements benefited only a few people. Apart from a small, urban middle class, most of the population continued to live in poverty and misery. Any form of protest was severely dealt with by the National Guard, which was formed in 1912.

It seemed things might improve with the election of Pio Romero Bosque in 1927, and of his successor Arturo Araujo, who promised democratic and social reform. But it was not to be. The Wall Street crash of 1929, followed by the Great Depression and the collapse of the world coffee market, plunged El Salvador into an even deeper crisis. At the time, coffee made up 95 percent of El Salvador's exports.

General Hernández Martínez, known as *El Brujo*

La Matanza

The first casualty of the crisis was President Araujo. In 1931, he was deposed in a military coup and replaced by General Maximiliano Hernández Martínez, nicknamed *El Brujo* (The Sorcerer). The military were particularly nervous of the newly formed Salvadoran Communist Party, led by university student Agustín Farabundo Martí, and the increasing unrest among peasants. The peasants suffered most from the lack of work and wages.

In January 1932, with the support of Farabundo Martí, Indian workers in the west rebelled. Armed mostly with machetes, they attacked military installations and assassinated civilians and government workers. The rebellion was easily crushed by government troops, and Farabundo Martí was caught and executed.

The government was not satisfied with these actions, and in order to firmly establish the role of the army alongside the powerful elite, a massacre followed. An estimated 10,000 people were killed. Never before had El Salvador known such repression. The army, the police, the private armies of the hacienda owners, and the National Guard began a full-scale persecution of the peasants. Whole communities were wiped out, and anyone recognizable as an Indian was shot. In fear, the Indians rejected their own culture, language, and traditional dress. From that time on, they assumed a mestizo way of life. The massacre, which became known as *La Matanza* (The Slaughter), was an early indication of the frightening lengths to which the wealthy and the army would go to retain power.

Military Rule

The military's iron rule of El Salvador continued for almost fifty years. They squabbled among themselves and there were many coups, but the armed forces held all the political power, and the wealthy people controlled the economy. Opposition to repression was difficult, particularly in the countryside, where labor organizations were illegal. The *campesinos*, or peasants, had no channels through which to make demands for better living and working conditions. Some political parties were permitted, but elections were a farce.

The military junta of Major Oscar Osorio in 1950 allowed some progressive projects, including the development of hydroelectric power and urban housing, but these mainly benefited the economy and the small middle class. The economy was still largely based on coffee, but sugar, cotton, and beef became important products after World War II. Some small-scale industry was producing manufactured goods for the local market. But none of this helped the great majority of the population, who continued to live in dreadful poverty.

Workers at a coffee factory in the 1950s

The Soccer War

In 1969, the *Guerra de Fútbol* (Soccer War) broke out between El Salvador and Honduras shortly after the two countries played three bad-tempered matches in the World Cup competition. The real reason for the conflict was a long-standing border dispute between the two countries. A large number of immigrants from El Salvador had settled illegally in Honduras. These immigrants were fleeing the bad times in El Salvador.

Honduras decided to send back about 300,000 people, who claimed they were badly treated. Acting on these claims, El Salvador went to war on July 14. The war lasted only two weeks, when pressure from the Organization of American States brought it to an end, but by that time several thousand people had been killed. A peace treaty between the two countries was not signed until 1980.

In the 1960s, members of political parties, business, and labor organizations proposed a large-scale redistribution of land, but they were ignored. The landowners simply did not want to hear them. According to the 1971 census, almost two-thirds of the land still belonged to just 4 percent of the population, while two-thirds of the peasants either had no land, or did not have enough to feed even themselves.

Resentment, frustration, and desperation all began to surface in the 1970s with the growing abuse of political and civil rights by the military. Fraudulent elections in 1972 kept the popular reform candidate José Napoleón Duarte of the Christian Democratic Party (PDC) out of power. His place was taken by the military candidate, Colonel Arturo Armando Molina. Duarte and some of his supporters were arrested, tortured, and exiled, and activists from trade unions and labor organizations were persecuted and killed.

There were endless acts of repression as antigovernment strikes, demonstrations, and parades increased. Some made headlines around the world, such as a group of college students

Archbishop Romero's
sermons gave new hope.

killed in 1975. They were protesting the use of public funds to hold the Miss Universe contest in El Salvador. And in early 1977, up to 300 unarmed civilians were killed during a protest in front of a cathedral. In the towns and countryside everywhere, death squads funded by the wealthy waged war against anyone who advocated reform. Elections were rigged again in 1977.

One voice that increasingly spoke out against the violence and demanded better conditions for the poor was that of the "reformed" Catholic Church. Once strictly conservative, the Catholic Church had adopted a new, concerned attitude toward the injustices and social deprivations of people in many parts of Latin America. In El Salvador, this attitude was expressed by Archbishop Oscar Romero, whose passionate Sunday sermons were heard on radio in every corner of the country. His sermons offered hope and support to all those fighting the military repression.

Among those fighting the government and the wealthy were several guerrilla organizations. In 1980, they were joined by the Communist Party. As a result of pressure from Fidel Castro at meetings in Cuba, the groups merged to become the Frente Faribundo Martí de Liberación Nacional (FMLN).

Civil War

Salvadorans protest a governing junta.

In 1979, military president Carlos Humberto Romero was deposed in a coup led by young army officers. The officers formed a civilian-military junta to govern El Salvador. They proposed an ambitious program of land reform and promised to end military rule and hold elections. They declared a political amnesty and invited the FMLN to participate, but fighting between the guerrillas and government troops continued.

The elections were postponed, but pressure from some progressive members of the government led to the formation of a second junta in 1980. It included the Christian Democrat leader José Napoleón Duarte, who returned home from exile. He joined the junta on condition that certain reforms be made, including the distribution of land. Duarte became president in December 1980.

Meanwhile, the wealthy, powerful families were beginning to realize that they could no longer rely on the military to protect their interests. They formed their own political party—The Nationalist Republican Alliance (ARENA)—led by Roberto D'Aubuisson Arrieta.

On March 24, 1980, the hugely popular Archbishop Oscar Romero was assassinated while saying Mass. It was later revealed that D'Aubuisson had organized the assassination. One act of violence led to another and culminated that year with the murder of three American nuns and a Roman Catholic lay worker by the military.

In January 1981, Ronald Reagan became president of the United States. Fiercely anticommunist, he viewed the guerrilla forces of the FMLN—along with the left-wing Sandinistas who held power in neighboring Nicaragua—as part of a cold war threat involving the Soviet Union and Cuba.

Also in January, the FMLN guerrillas organized their first military offensive and gained territory in north and east El Salvador. Following these gains, the FDR, a political party allied with the FMLN, proposed negotiations with the United States, who in turn referred them to the Salvadoran government. However, the

Catholic women killed by the military in 1980

The Massacre of El Mozote

Hoping to break up guerrilla strongholds in the north, the Salvadoran army organized Operation Rescue. In December 1981, it carried out probably the most horrific massacre of the war. The killing took place in El Mozote (right), a mountain village inhabited by many born-again Christians. The village itself was not a guerrilla center, but it lay in the heart of what the army termed the "Red Zone." More than 1,000 civilians were killed in the massacre. Very few people escaped.

government refused to meet with the FDR while it was linked with the guerrillas. President Reagan and the U.S. government affirmed their support for the Duarte government by supplying financial, technical, and military aid.

From that time, it was open warfare between the two sides—the military and the wealthy elite supported by the United States against the guerrillas backed by the Soviet Union, Mexico, Cuba, and Nicaragua. The civil war lasted until 1992 and took more than 75,000 lives. Another 70,000 people were injured, and more than 500,000 fled the country as refugees. In all, up to 1 million people—one-fifth of the population—were forced from their homes.

Political developments had little impact on the war. Elections in 1982 led to the formation of a Government of

Roberto D'Aubuisson Arrieta

National Unity in which the key player was D'Aubuisson Arrieta, the right-wing leader of ARENA. A new Constitution was drawn up in 1983, and some 1,600 Salvadoran troops were sent to train in the United States.

Early in 1984, after the guerrillas had gained some additional territory, the FDR-FMLN proposed the formation of a broadly based government as part of a peace plan. When the plan was rejected, the guerrillas refused to take part in the March elections. José Napoleón Duarte was elected president. Talks between the two sides after the election held out hope for some reconciliation, but they were unable to negotiate an end to the conflict. The war went on and the country suffered.

Toward the end of the 1980s, peace seemed a long way off. Early in 1989, however, the guerrillas announced that they would be willing to take part in the next elections. They asked for a postponement of the elections for six months and offered to call for a cease-fire for thirty days before and after the elections. Their offer was refused, and the FMLN intensified its military campaign. The day Alfredo Cristiani Burkard of the ARENA Party was elected president, the FMLN killed forty people.

Beginning in August 1989, meetings were held by the heads of state of several Central American countries, urging the FMLN to join the talks. A bomb attack apparently carried out by the army killed ten people in the Salvadoran Workers' National Union Federation, however, and the violence escalated. Late that year, there was international outrage when the military massacred six Jesuit priests, their housekeeper, and her daughter on the campus of the University of Central America in San Salvador.

But a move toward peace had become part of the agenda. The Salvadoran people were weary of war, and the guerrillas had increasing reason to recognize the superior armed power of the military. At the same time, the military knew that a stalemate could last for years. The United States, too, was tiring of the conflict. After having spent some U.S.$6 billion on it, the U.S. Congress was calling for a cut in military aid to El Salvador. There was public outrage in North America when a U.S. military helicopter en route to Honduras was shot down by Salvadoran guerrilla forces, who subsequently executed two of the servicemen who had survived the crash.

The most significant event to affect the course of the war was the collapse of the Soviet Union and the end of the cold war. The thawing of relations between Russia and the United States put the communist threat in El Salvador in a different perspective. It also meant that Cuba and Nicaragua no longer had the resources to support the FMLN. Peace talks resumed early in 1991.

The Chapultepec Peace Accords

After many months of negotiations and wrangling, peace accords were signed in Chapultepec in Mexico City on

In Remembrance

A small rose garden in the grounds of the University of Central America commemorates the lives of Archbishop Oscar Romero and the six Jesuit priests, their housekeeper, her daughter, and other human-rights workers who died in El Salvador's civil war. A circle of bushes surrounds a statue representing the archbishop. In a nearby museum, volunteers guide visitors around the photos, personal effects, and mementos of these greatly revered victims.

January 16, 1992. The United Nations played a vital role in persuading the opposing forces to reach agreement. The accords not only marked the official end of the war but also secured agreements for the FMLN affecting the future role of the military in Salvadoran society and several other important issues. In return, the FMLN agreed to give up their weapons and promised to become part of the legitimate political process.

Under the accords, military strength would be cut in half, and officers found responsible for the worst human-rights abuses would be dismissed. A newly created National Civilian Police would be responsible for public security and would include former members of the FMLN. The accords also determined that the courts should be less politically oriented and judges should be elected on a more fair basis. An independent government organization would see that human rights were respected. Elections should be democratic, and the FMLN and other opposition groups would be accepted as legitimate political parties and their rights guaranteed.

Although economic problems—especially land reform— contributed in large part to the guerrillas taking up arms in the first place, the accords dealt with these issues in much less detail. It was determined that troops on both sides should be integrated into the national economy, and that land would be transferred to some 40,000 guerrillas and civilian supporters of the FMLN. Both sides agreed to pursue further economic changes as needed, through the new political system. The United Nations set up a resident observer mission to monitor progress.

The Truth Commission

At an early stage in the negotiations that led to the peace accords, it was agreed that a *Comisión de la Verdad* (Truth Commission) should be established to look into the worst atrocities of the civil war. The commission published its report, entitled "From Madness to Hope: Twelve Years of War in El Salvador," in March 1993. It found that the vast majority of the war's 75,000 fatalities were the result of the military forces carrying out anti-guerrilla activities. Their activities included mass murders of anyone thought to be associated with or supporting the left-wing fighters.

More than 200 military personnel were alleged to have taken part in abuses of human rights, and 40 were specifically

General René Emilio Ponce

named. They included the Minister of Defense and Public Security General René Emilio Ponce and his deputy, who with other members of the high command ordered the murders of the six priests and others in 1989. Major Roberto D'Aubuisson (who had died of cancer in 1992) was singled out as the man who organized the death squads and the assassination of Archbishop Romero. The Atlacatl Battalion, which had completed its training under the supervision of U.S. military advisers, was said to be responsible for the El Mozote massacre. The FMLN were accused of some 400 murders between 1985 and 1988, including those of many rural mayors.

Nor did the United States escape censure. Throughout the war, the U.S. government supported the wealthy civilians and the military by training troops and providing weapons and other technical aid. The United States also donated huge sums of financial aid—more than U.S.$1 million per day by the mid-1980s—to prevent a communist takeover of El Salvador. The commission accused the U.S. government of ignoring Salvadoran human rights in its desire to defeat the guerrillas.

The Truth Commission recommended that anyone named in the report be dismissed from his military or government post. It also recommended that all the justices of the Supreme Court resign. Finally, the report recognized and condemned the support given to the death squads by wealthy civilians and called for action to prevent the forming of such groups in future.

Predictably enough, while the FMLN welcomed the report, others rejected it. The Supreme Court justices refused to resign, the military refused to acknowledge the findings, and ARENA called the report "biased." Within a week, ARENA pushed an amnesty law through the Legislative Assembly for all the accused. The public was outraged.

Elections of the Century

In 1994, for the first time after the civil war, elections were held for the presidency, the Legislative Assembly, and for the country's 262 mayors. The elections were also significant because the FMLN was participating for the first time as a political party. Its presidential candidate was Rubén Zamora, a left-wing intellectual who also had the support of the Democratic Convergence (CD) party.

Election posters in El Salvador

The campaign got off to a bad start when an illegal armed group gunned down three prominent FMLN candidates. After the United Nations stepped in, violence gave way to a relatively peaceful campaign. The elections in March were inconclusive. In an April run-off election, ARENA candidate Armando Calderón Sol beat Zamora with 68.2 percent of the votes.

ARENA also gained control in the Legislative Assembly and won 206 of the 262 municipal elections. But by winning 22 of the 84 seats in the Legislative Assembly, the FMLN established itself as a respectable political party.

El Salvador Today

Discontent is growing in El Salvador because the government has failed to honor the terms of the peace accords. Some military officers have been dismissed, but few have been brought to justice. Most have been offered amnesty or early retirement. The National Civilian Police has been unable to do its job due to lack of funds, and some former troops and refugees have received neither the land nor the financial compensation they were promised. Corruption is still widespread, and frustration has led former soldiers and others to stage protests and demonstrations.

Elections in 1997 for the Legislative Assembly and municipal mayors led to unexpected gains for the FMLN. In the Legislative Assembly, ARENA won twenty-nine seats, just two more than the FMLN, and the FMLN candidate was elected mayor of San Salvador.

Despite hopes raised by this FMLN success, the 1999 presidential elections were won by Francisco Flores Perez of the ARENA Party. A graduate of Amherst College and former philosophy professor, Flores faces many challenges to restore confidence and stability in El Salvador.

President Perez meets well-wishers.

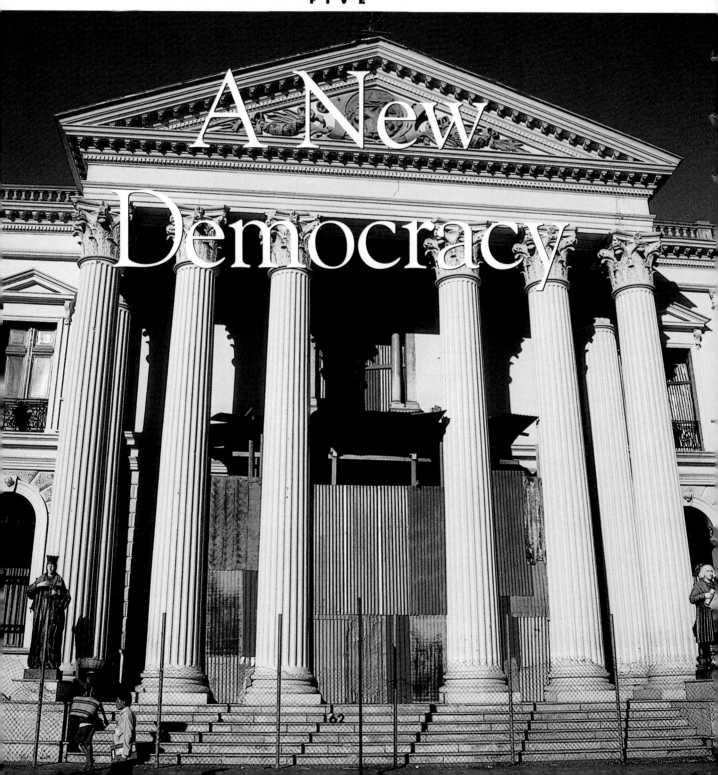

CHAPTER

FIVE

A New
Democracy

E L Salvador's Constitution was drawn up in 1983 and amended in 1992. According to the Constitution, the national government should be democratic and consist of executive, legislative, and judicial branches. Everyone over the age of eighteen is expected to vote.

The executive branch is headed by the president, who is elected to a five-year term beginning and ending on June 1. The president must leave office at the end of that five-year term and cannot be reelected. If no candidate secures an absolute majority after the first round of voting, a run-off election takes place between the top two candidates. If the president dies or is removed during his or her term, his place is taken by the vice president.

Opposite: **The National Palace**

The National Flag

El Salvador's flag, adopted on September 15, 1912, consists of a white band between two horizontal blue bands. The national coat of arms, centered in the white band, was created by the Salvadoran calligrapher Rafael Barraza Rodriguez. The three parts of an equilateral triangle are said to represent Liberty, Equality, and Fraternity. The emblem features five volcanoes; two oceans, the Atlantic and the Pacific; a rainbow with the colors of the Central American federation; and fourteen laurel branches that represent the country's fourteen departments. At the base of one of the branches are the Spanish words for God, Union, and Freedom.

José Napoleón Duarte

José Napoleón Duarte was born in 1925, the son of a tailor. He was educated at the Catholic Liceo Salvadoreño. Active in student politics from an early age, in 1944 he took part in a general strike against the dictatorship of General Maximiliano Hernández Martínez. He earned a degree in civil engineering from Notre Dame University in the United States, married, and had six children. In 1960, Duarte joined the Christian Democrat Party, then in its infancy. His political career took off when he was elected mayor of San Salvador. He gained a good reputation and was reelected twice. In February 1972, he ran for president, but amid widespread allegations of fraud, the military-backed candidate was declared the winner. Duarte became involved in a coup and was arrested and sent into exile.

Between 1980 and 1982, Duarte, who had returned from exile, served as president of a new civilian-military junta. Despite his own torture at the hands of the military, and their part in the increasing violence of the early 1980s, Duarte continued to work with them even after his election as president in 1984. He raised hopes of an end to the civil war by beginning a dialogue with the FMLN guerrillas, but nothing came of the talks. In the 1988 elections, Duarte suffered a humiliating defeat by Alfredo Cristiani, the ARENA candidate. He died early in 1990.

El Salvador's Legislative Assembly building

In addition to the president and the vice president, there is a cabinet known as the Council of Ministers. The executive branch is responsible for the preparation of the budget, foreign affairs, and organization of the armed forces and the security forces.

El Salvador has a one-house Legislative Assembly with eighty-four members who are elected every three years, for terms beginning on May 1. Sixty-four of the members are elected as representatives of El Salvador's fourteen departments, and the other twenty are elected on a proportional basis nationwide.

The Supreme Court is the highest court in the land. It is composed of fourteen magistrates who are elected by a two-thirds majority of the Legislative Assembly. The Supreme Court has the power to appoint and—if necessary—remove local judges.

Local government is based on 14 departments and 262 municipalities. Each municipality is headed by a mayor who is elected by the people.

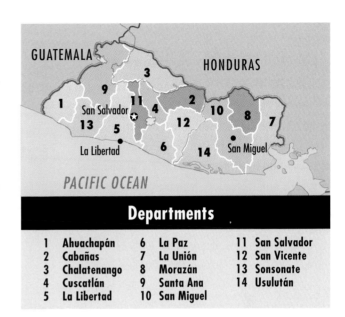

Departments

1	Ahuachapán	6	La Paz	11	San Salvador
2	Cabañas	7	La Unión	12	San Vicente
3	Chalatenango	8	Morazán	13	Sonsonate
4	Cuscatlán	9	Santa Ana	14	Usulután
5	La Libertad	10	San Miguel		

NATIONAL GOVERNMENT OF EL SALVADOR

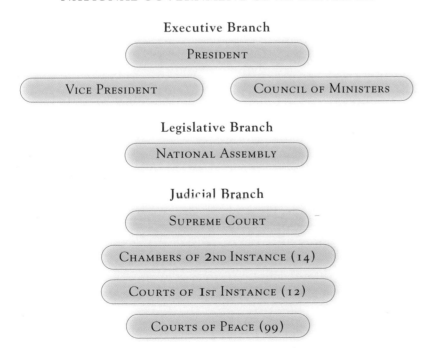

Executive Branch

PRESIDENT

VICE PRESIDENT

COUNCIL OF MINISTERS

Legislative Branch

NATIONAL ASSEMBLY

Judicial Branch

SUPREME COURT

CHAMBERS OF 2ND INSTANCE (14)

COURTS OF 1ST INSTANCE (12)

COURTS OF PEACE (99)

San Salvador: Did You Know This?

In 1525, Pedro de Alvarado founded San Salvador in the Las Hamacas Valley in the southern mountains. From 1834 to 1838, it was the capital of the United Provinces of Central America. Since 1839, the city has been the capital of the independent Republic of El Salvador. The nation's leading commercial, industrial, and transportation center, San Salvador was home to 422,570 people in 1995.

San Salvador stands along the Río Ace Chaute at an altitude of 2,162 feet (659 m), less than 19 miles (30 km) from the Pacific Ocean. The temperature varies little around the year, averaging 71°F (22°C) in January and 75°F (24°C) in July. Average annual rainfall is 71 inches (180 cm). Major earthquakes have damaged San Salvador several times, most recently in 2001.

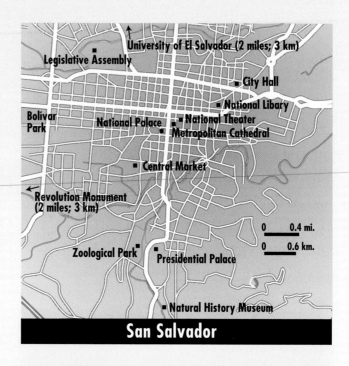

San Salvador

Before the election, each person running for mayor names a prospective team of officials. All of these officials take their place alongside the successful candidate for mayor.

Political Parties

Nine political parties were represented in the Legislative Assembly after the 1997 elections:

- ARENA (Nationalist Republican Alliance); the ruling, right-wing party
- CD (Democratic Convergence); a coalition of small, left-wing parties
- FMLN (Farabundo Martí National Liberation Front); former left-wing guerrilla group that was legally recognized in 1992
- MU (Unity Movement); evangelical party founded in 1993
- PCN (National Conciliation Party); right-wing party formed in 1961 and associated with the military
- PDC (Christian Democratic Party); reformist party composed mainly of middle- and working-class people
- PDC/PD (Democratic Party); center-left breakaway group of the Christian Democrats
- PLD (Democratic Liberal Party); founded in 1991
- PRSC (Social Christian Renovation Party)

The National Anthem

The *himno nacional* (national anthem) was written and composed by Juan Aberle, an Italian who arrived in El Salvador toward the end of the nineteenth century, and General Juan José Canas, a poet. Entitled *"Saludemos la patria orgullosos"* ("We Proudly Salute the Fatherland"), it was first performed September 1879.

Rebuilding the Economy

Uring the 1980s, El Salvador's economy was devastated by civil war. Guerrilla attacks destroyed many agricultural areas, power installations, and roads. The October 1986 earthquake also destroyed housing and government property, and it caused business losses valued at around U.S.$2 billion. As if this were not trouble enough, two years later a hurricane brought further destruction, and continuing droughts also had a severe effect.

Throughout most of this period, El Salvador depended heavily on financial aid from the United States. In the mid-1980s, U.S. aid payments made up one-half of El Salvador's national budget.

In 1989, President Alfredo Cristiani and the new government introduced a national rescue plan. It was designed to reduce public spending while providing jobs, food, and low-cost housing for those people most in need. The government also wanted to reduce inflation, encourage exports, privatize businesses, and attract foreign investment. International organizations including the World Bank, the International Monetary Fund, and the Inter-American Development Bank approved Cristiani's policies and agreed to loan the Salvadoran government millions of dollars.

After the end of the civil war in 1992, loans and substantial amounts of aid were also available to support a plan of national

Opposite: **A family harvesting watermelons**

reconstruction. That plan involved a wide range of programs including agricultural and medical training; helping former soldiers find a place in society; re-integrating "guerrilla" areas of the country; and re-building towns, roads, bridges, and the many installations damaged or destroyed during the war.

In 1990, the growth rate of El Salvador's economy was just 1 percent. By the end of Cristiani's term in 1994, it was 6 percent, and inflation had slowed. This progress continued during the Armando administration of Calderón Sol, although it was due more to a postwar construction boom and demand for consumer goods than to any fundamental changes in the economy. By 1997, El Salvador was able to attract more foreign and private investment, and the government was able to secure more international loans.

U.S. president Bill Clinton meets with Armando Calderón Sol.

Agriculture

El Salvador's greatest assets are its rich soil, moderate climate, and hardworking people. Throughout its history, agriculture has been the basis of the Salvadoran economy—first cacao, followed by indigo, and then coffee. Today, the main agricultural exports are coffee, sugar, and shrimp. In 1995, more than one-fourth of the working population were involved in agriculture, which also includes fishing and forestry.

These women are cleaning coffee.

What El Salvador Grows, Makes, and Mines	
Agriculture (1996)	
Sugarcane	3,900,000 metric tons
Corn (maize)	639,600 metric tons
Sorghum	109,600 metric tons
Manufacturing (1995) *(valued added in colones)*	
Food products	2,807,000,000 value added
Chemical products	854,000,000 value added
Beverages	837,000,000 value added
Mining (1993)	
Limestone	2,600,000 metric tons

In the 1920s, coffee accounted for almost 95 percent of El Salvador's exports. Until the civil war, Salvadoran coffee production was considered the most efficient in Central America. After Brazil, Colombia, and Mexico, El Salvador was the fourth-largest coffee producer in Latin America. But the industry dived during the 1980s. It has revived since the mid-1990s, helped by bad weather in Brazil that led to an increase in world coffee prices. In 1996, coffee accounted for almost one-third of Salvadoran export earnings, and today El Salvador is the world's third-largest coffee producer.

Cotton, once an important export, was also badly affected by the war. Farms in the rural areas were attacked by guerrilla forces. No longer able to afford the chemicals and machinery needed to process cotton crops, the industry is now very small.

Sugar and shrimp are two other important products. Sugar is grown for sale to both local and foreign markets, and it also provides seasonal cane-cutting work in rural areas. The government has built shrimp farms along the coast that employ the local people and produce enough shrimp for export. El Salvador has attempted to diversify its agricultural exports by introducing crops such as soybeans, honey, melons, cucumbers, and ornamental plants. It also has a small tobacco industry.

People working on a shrimp farm

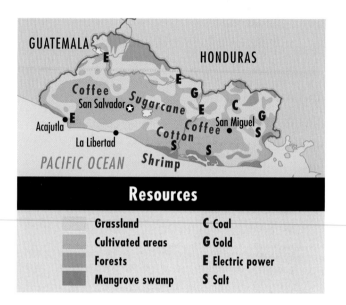

Resources

▨ Grassland		**C** Coal
▨ Cultivated areas		**G** Gold
▨ Forests		**E** Electric power
▨ Mangrove swamp		**S** Salt

During the 1980s, when meat was scarce, a poultry industry developed. Today, El Salvador exports eggs and broiler chickens to neighboring countries. Other aspects of the agricultural industry are cattle-ranching and forestry. Some woods are used to make furniture, but the main forest products are logwood and balsam, a medicinal resin.

In rural El Salvador, families grow many of their own crops, including maize, beans, and rice and most keep a few animals. Most fruits and vegetables are imported from Guatemala.

Manufacturing

Manufacturing in El Salvador got a major boost with the formation of the Central American Common Market in 1960. It opened up a huge market of some 10 million people and cut taxes on goods passing between the member countries—Guatemala, El Salvador, Honduras, Nicaragua, and Costa Rica. Industrial plants were built throughout the country, and manufacturing became the fastest-growing sector of the economy.

The civil war affected manufacturing during the 1980s. It damaged factories, electric power plants, and transportation networks, and a lack of currency reduced the demand for goods. Since then, however, manufacturing has bounced back, and El Salvador is the most industrialized of the Central American

Balsam

Balsam is a medicinal resin from a tropical tree. Balsam and El Salvador go hand in hand. The substance, used centuries ago as a medicine, was taken to Europe by the Spanish. They mistakenly named it "Balsam of Peru." In El Salvador, *balsameros* (resin collectors) work from December to June, making cuts in the bark that allow the resin to ooze out. Even as recently as the mid-1940s, annual balsam production was in the region of 90 tons, but with the development of synthetic medicines, demand for the natural product declined. The balsam tree grows to a height of around 40 feet (12 m). Every October, a Balsam Festival is held in Santa Tecla.

countries. Its most important manufactured products are processed food and drinks, prepared drugs, aluminum, paper, and paperboard products. Textiles, chemicals, cement, plastics, cigarettes, shoes, and leather goods are also manufactured.

The most rapid development in manufacturing has been the Free Zone *maquila* industry. Here, hundreds of people work in *maquiladoras* (export assembly plants) owned by both foreign and Salvadoran companies. In these plants, almost everything—including all imported materials and machinery—is tax-free. El Salvador provides the large numbers of people, especially women, who work long hours for little pay, often in grim conditions. Most maquiladoras in El Salvador produce clothing items.

Workers sewing clothing in a maquiladora

Money Old and New

El Salvador's traditional monetary unit is the *colón*. There are 100 *centavos* in each colón. Bank notes are issued in denominations of 5, 10, 25, and 100 colones; coins, as 5, 10, 25, and 50 centavos.

The figure on the front of the 5-colón note is Christopher Columbus. In Spanish, he is known as Cristobal Colón, and the Salvadoran currency is named after him. Also pictured are the three ships in which Columbus sailed to America for the first time in 1492—the *Niña*, the *Pinta*, and the *Santa María*. On the back of the 5-colón note is the *Palacio Nacional* (National Palace). It symbolizes the government in El Salvador and the hope of a peaceful, democratic future.

In January 2001, under the new Monetary Integration Law, El Salvador began using U.S. dollars instead of colones. The government hopes a dollar-based economy will stimulate economic growth and lower national interest rates. Some Salvadorans have protested this change.

Sending Money Home

During the civil war, more than 1 million Salvadorans left the country. About half settled in the United States, while others went to Canada, Australia, Europe, Mexico, and other parts of Central America. They found work and began sending money home to their families. The sums grew so large that they exceeded the annual earnings from coffee exports, and later totaled more than all of El Salvador's export earnings. The total for 1999 was expected to reach U.S.$1.4 billion.

This dollar revenue continues today. It is vital to keeping the country's economy stable, and to offset its large trade deficit. So it is not surprising that the Salvadoran government is anxious about the status of Salvadoran immigrants in the United States. The Salvadorans have asked the U.S. government to allow them to stay, but until final decisions are made, they could be sent back to El Salvador at any time.

Natural Resources

El Salvador has few mineral resources. There are gold and silver in the mountains of Morazán, and limestone and sea salt are quarried. The main source of power is hydro-electricity.

Workers store sea salt.

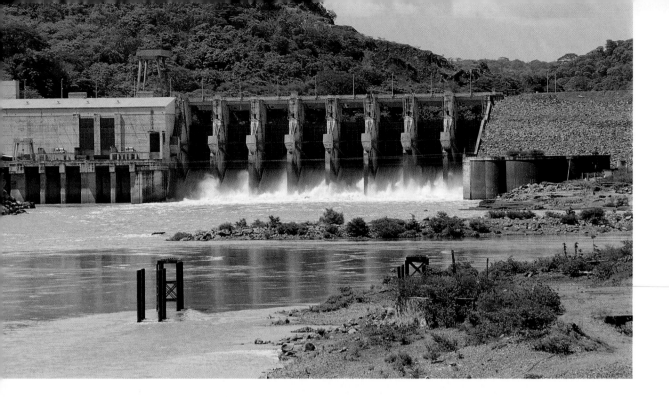

A dam on the Río Lempa

Four dams provide less than half the country's power needs. The largest dam is on the Río Lempa, not far from San Salvador. El Salvador has to import oil to make up much of the remaining energy needs. In rural areas, wood is commonly used for fuel.

A Shopping List From 2001

In 2001, 8.76 colones was equal to U.S.$1. So each colon (¢) was worth about 11 1/2 cents. Here are some typical prices:

Soft drink (1 can)	¢5	Movie ticket	¢30
Toothpaste (medium tube)	¢15	Water container	¢1
Toilet paper (1 roll)	¢3	Water (1 liter)	¢7
Newspaper	¢2	French bread (small)	¢1
City bus ride	¢1	Entry to museum/ruins	¢25
Four-hour bus ride	¢6	Mosquito coils	¢9
Packet of candles	¢5	Pupusas (corn snacks)	¢3
Meal at McDonalds	¢30	Machete	¢7

Transport

Despite the damage done to the transport network during the civil war, El Salvador has a reasonably good road system. Two main routes of the Pan American Highway cross El Salvador from Guatemala to Honduras—one through the central plain, the other along the coast. Paved, all-weather roads connect these main highways to most outlying areas, and it takes only hours to get from one end of the country to another.

The Pan American Highway as it crosses El Salvador

Tankers at port in Acajutla

El Salvador has three main ports on the Pacific coast—Acajutla, La Libertad, and Puerto Cutuco—and one on the Atlantic coast through Guatemala's Puerto Barrios. San Salvador is linked to its Atlantic port by road and rail via Guatemala City.

Land Reform

From colonial times, the wealthy ruling class owned most of the land in El Salvador and controlled the economy. About 70 percent of the nation's farmers were laborers on large plantations living in servile, miserable conditions. The first, modest, attempt at agricultural reform began in 1976, during the rule of President Arturo Molina. It was an effort to redistribute the land more fairly, so that the landless peasants would have a small share. The reaction from the large landowners, including the use of death squads to murder peasants, was so hostile that Molina gave up the plan, however.

In 1980, the junta led by José Duarte produced the Land Reform Law. Only the first phase of the law was ever implemented. In this phase, farms exceeding 1,235 acres (500 ha) were broken up and handed over to peasant cooperative groups. The cooperatives were made up primarily of families who had worked on these estates. Some 20 percent of the land was redistributed to more than 85,000 *campesinos*, or peasants. From the start, the cooperatives faced an immense struggle. During the war years, they had to find ways of dealing with financial and technical problems. They, too, became the targets of death squads, and many cooperative leaders were murdered.

Land reform was an essential part of the 1992 Chapultepec Peace Accords. The government agreed to redistribute the land of all estates larger than 600 acres (243 ha). It also agreed to give land to about 40,000 former soldiers from both sides, including people who had effectively "squatted," or farmed land abandoned during the war. The plan got off to a slow start with shortages of funds and complex bureaucracy, and by mid-1993 little more than half of the land had been distributed.

In February 1996, the U.S. government provided U.S.$10 million for the completion of the program. It remains to be seen whether the rest of the land will be transferred to the former guerrillas and government soldiers.

System of Weights and Measures

The metric system is the official system of weights and measures, but some old Spanish measures are also commonly used. For example, 1 *libra* is equal to 1.014 pounds (about 0.45 kg), and 1 *quintal* equals 100 pounds (45.36 kg).

Salvadorans

Decline of the Indians

Eʟ Sᴀʟᴠᴀᴅᴏʀ ʜᴀꜱ ᴀ ᴘᴏᴘᴜʟᴀᴛɪᴏɴ ᴏꜰ ᴀʙᴏᴜᴛ 6 ᴍɪʟʟɪᴏɴ, with an average of about 700 people per square mile of land (270 per sq km). Only about 5 percent of today's people are pure Indians. After the Spanish conquest, thousands of Indians died of ill treatment and disease. Eventually, mixed-race *mestizos* born of Spanish and Indian parents outnumbered the pure Indian population.

In recent times, most of the remaining Indians have rejected their culture and customs for fear of persecution. Today, only small numbers of Izalco and Pancho people survive. The Pancho come from the village of Panchimalco, near San Salvador. There is little to identify them as Indians—perhaps a glimpse of the traditional colorful, striped skirts with white or colored blouses worn by the women, or the few elderly people who speak Nahuatl, or the occasional fiesta. The vibrant Indian life typical of their neighbors in Guatemala is no longer present.

Opposite: **An El Salvadoran woman carrying a basket of food**

Panchimalco is a village of Pancho Indians.

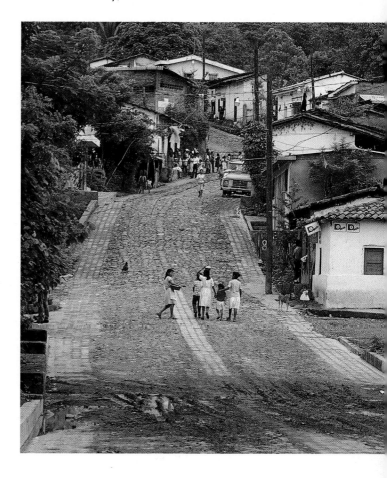

Population of Major Cities (1995 est.)	
San Salvador	422,570
Santa Ana	202,337
San Miguel	182,817
Nueva San Salvador	116,575
Ahuachapán	83,885

Mestizos and Ladinos

Most Salvadorans are mestizos, except for the tiny group of people directly descended from European families and small numbers of Palestinian, Lebanese, and Jewish immigrants from the Middle East. In El Salvador and other Central American countries, the word *ladino* is widely used to describe a person—European, mestizo, or Indian—who has adopted Spanish-American culture and speaks Spanish.

A woman of Palestinian descent working in El Salvador

Who Lives in El Salvador?	
Mestizos	94 %
Indians	5 %
Caucasians	1 %

Women selling food on a city street

Salvadoran society is still one of the most unequal in Latin America. While the elite continue to have a lifestyle similar to that of wealthy people in developed countries, the poor remain largely unemployed, uneducated, in poor health, and malnourished. In rural areas, many families still have no land and lack the most basic facilities. Little work is available, except on plantations and some seasonal farm-work.

Desperate for a better way of life, scores of rural Salvadorans daily make their way to the towns. To their disappointment, they find that things are seldom any better there. In some urban centers, up to 50 percent of the people are unemployed. Many families eke out a living by selling food and trinkets on the streets or doing odd jobs such as washing cars or running errands. Some find domestic work as maids or

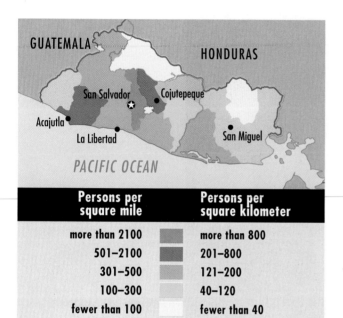

Persons per square mile		Persons per square kilometer
more than 2100		more than 800
501–2100		201–800
301–500		121–200
100–300		40–120
fewer than 100		fewer than 40

gardeners, or share a car to run a taxi service. Others enlist in the military, and some find jobs in factories.

A middle class has been slow to develop in El Salvador. Only about 10 percent of mestizos are employed in professional work, mostly as doctors, lawyers, teachers, and government workers.

The Role of Women

Women have an ambiguous role in Salvadoran society. During the civil war, they fought in the front line with the FMLN and shared many tasks

Say It in Spanish

Spanish is El Salvador's official language. Native languages are virtually extinct, despite government and university efforts to preserve the Nahuatl language.

The Spanish alphabet has 28 letters. It does not have k or w, but does include the letters *ch, ll, ñ* and *rr.* Spanish vowels have a single sound and are always pronounced the same way:

a as in *car*
e as in *pet*
i as in *seek*
o as in *toe*
u as in *rude*

Consonants are similar to those in English but with some exceptions:

1. *b* and *v* sound the same
2. *c* is like "s" before *e* and *i*
3. *d* within a word is pronounced "th," except after "l" and "n," when it is like the "d" in *desk*
4. *ch* is pronounced as in *chair*
5. *h* is not pronounced in Spanish
6. *j* has no exact equivalent in English, but is similar to the "h" in *happy*
7. *ll* is similar to the "y" in *yacht*
8. *ñ* is pronounced "ny" like the "ni" in *onion*
9. *qu* replaces the "k" sound
10. *rr* is strongly rolled

Women training as soldiers

with men. Thousands of women died, both as fighters and as civilian casualties. So the survivors had reason to hope that men would continue to respect their position after the war, and that the days of all-powerful, macho men and the abuse of women might be over. But this is not the case. Sadly, domestic violence is widespread today.

So many men died or abandoned their families during the war that women now head more than half the households in El Salvador. They do what they can to survive. In the countryside, they cultivate small plots of land, while in the cities, most families trading on the streets are headed by women. Some women work as domestic servants or in factories, where they work long hours for low wages. For example, female machinists in a *maquiladora* may take home about $U.S.25 for a fifty-hour workweek. It is barely enough to keep a family going, but most women consider themselves fortunate to have a job at all.

A woman working at a computer in a modern office

Since the end of the war, most women have been expected to return to their traditional roles. But many women resent this situation and have formed movements to promote the needs of women, especially poor women. They have also shown that with a good education, women can do well in the professions. About half the country's dentists and teachers and one-third of its lawyers and doctors are women today.

Return of the Refugees

Some of the many thousands of people who fled from El Salvador during the war found refuge in camps across

Members of a refugee family carry their belongings.

the border in Honduras. One camp, Colomoncagua, housed many refugees from the Morazán region of northern El Salvador. In a few years, the refugees created a well-organized, unified society though they had no land to cultivate and lived on financial aid from international agencies. The Honduran government did not allow them to trade, but they set up workshops, repair shops, and other services that the local Hondurans used.

In 1989, even before the war ended, the refugees decided they wanted to return home, back to the land where the terrible El Mozote massacre and others had taken place. Over a period of four months, some 8,000 refugees made the trek. They carried with them every nut, screw, bolt, and plank of wood, plus all the equipment they had used to create the Colomoncagua camp.

The Honduran side of the border has pretty villages and well-cultivated land. But in Morazán, much of the land is barren, and the only bridge connecting northern Morazán to the south was destroyed by the military. The refugees

Popular Expressions

In El Salvador, many popular expressions are in daily use. Salvadorans, for example, call themselves *guanacos*, and a popular Salvadoran saying is known as a *guanaquidiom*. Here are a few expressions with their English translation and interpretation:

Al Chucho mas flaco se le pegan las pulgas.
("The skinniest dog gets the fleas.")
The weakest person gets the blame.

caerse de la moto
("To fall off the motorcycle")
To fall out of favor/not to be liked anymore.

En boca cerrada no entran moscas.
("A closed mouth gathers no flies.")
It pays to be discreet.

paja, pura paja, o hablar paja
("straw," "just straw," or "to talk pure straw")
To talk nonsense, or, more precisely, to tell lies.

Al que quiera celeste, que le cueste.
("He who wants a blue sky has to work for it.")
If you want results, you have to work for them.

Indio comido al camino.
("Indian who has eaten, to the road.")
To a visitor who has had lunch, etc.: Time to hit the road.

El diablo paso la cola.
("The devil's tail passed by.")
A bad atmosphere, where people begin to quarrel.

Me dejo silvando en la loma.
("He/she left me whistling on the hill.")
He/she stood me up.

created their own community, which they called *Ciudad Segundo Montes*. It is named for a Jesuit priest who was assassinated at the University of Central America. He had been a friend and supporter of the refugees while they were living in Colomoncagua.

Children playing at Ciudad Segundo Montes

Ciudad Segundo Montes is now a community of five settlements with schools, medical clinics, workshops, stores, and chapels. Much of the construction was paid for with money from international-aid agencies, but the refugees have created an economy from which they can earn money. For now, this comes mainly from workshops that make wood and metal objects, including chairs and desks for schools, and domestic items, such as galvanized-iron bowls and buckets. Their clothing and shoe factories have won contracts to supply the new national police force.

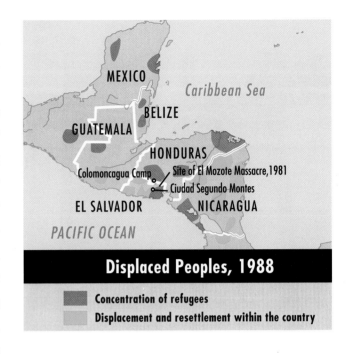

Displaced Peoples, 1988

Concentration of refugees

Displacement and resettlement within the country

Land remains a serious problem, however. Most families grow their own vegetables and fruit in a *parcela*, or kitchen garden, and a *milpa*, or cornfield. But with virtually all the land cultivated, there is none left over for growing crops for sale.

The development of this community has not been without problems, especially between workers and the small but powerful political group that runs the community. For the most part, however, the two sides have worked together to create a base and—they hope—a future for their children. More than half the population of Ciudad Segundo Montes is under fourteen years old.

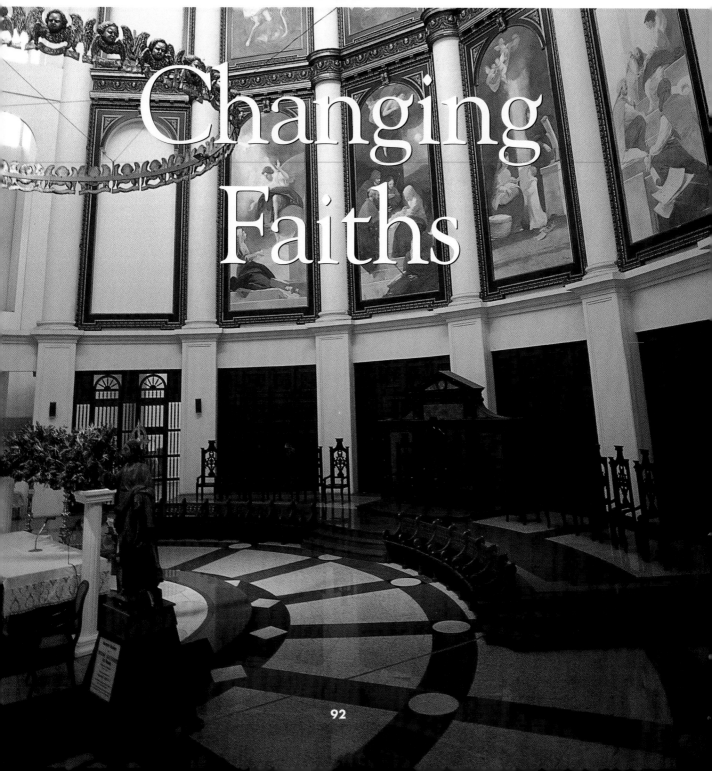

Changing Faiths

THE FIRST HUNTER-GATHERERS WHO SETTLED IN THE region that is now El Salvador found it to be a plentiful land. They enjoyed an abundance of wild food, and it did not take the people long to begin farming, too. Maize was the staple of their daily diet, and the life-giving sky and earth were key to their spiritual world.

Colonial Churches in El Salvador

The first formal religion began in Mayan times. With it came astronomy, a calendar, and a powerful priesthood. When the Spaniards arrived from Europe, they brought their own religion—the Roman Catholic faith. The people soon began to weave Catholicism into the fabric of their existing beliefs. Churches replaced temples, Mass replaced ritual offerings, and the people's allegiance was directed from local spirits to one new and powerful god.

Holy week procession in Nahuizalco

The passage of time has long since eradicated many of the ancient beliefs. Most of the remaining Indians live in the western provinces, particularly around Izalco Volcano. There, the small town of Nahuizalco becomes crowded

Cojutepeque

One of the most famous Catholic shrines in El Salvador is set on a hill beside Cojutepeque, a small town east of San Salvador. Known as the "City of Mists" for the heavy fog that covers it most afternoons, the town has a long history dating from pre-Spanish times. Spaniards settled there in 1659, and the hill, which was revered by the Indians, became a place of pilgrimage.

The shrine is named for Our Lady of Fátima, usually associated with poor children. The story began in the small Portuguese town of Fátima. There, on May 13, 1917, three poor children saw a vision of a woman. The vision appeared five times. The last time, the "Lady" told the children to recite the rosary every day. The statue in

Cojutepeque was brought from Fátima in 1949. It is visited by crowds of pilgrims every year on May 13.

for the festival of Saint John the Baptist in June, when processions and Catholic Mass are accompanied by colorful dances. In neighboring Sonsonate, the festival of *Candelaria*, or Candlemas, is celebrated from late January and continues to February 2. These festivals blend the traditions of the Catholic Church with folklore from times past expressing the conflict of good and evil spirits.

Important Religious Holidays

Holy Week	March or April
Easter Sunday	March or April
Corpus Christi	June
El Salvador del Mundo	August 3–6
All Souls' Day	November 2
Virgin of Guadalupe	December 12
Christmas	December 25–31

The Church and Politics

With very few exceptions, the Catholic priesthood and the power of the Roman Catholic Church in Latin America were controlled by the wealthy and the powerful for more than 400 years. Rich people hoping for even greater influence gave money to the church, poor artisans built the churches, and the Indians were simply onlookers. But the rapidly changing politics of the world in the 1950s and 1960s led many Catholic priests to reconsider their role in society. They decided to help the growing numbers of poor people. Naturally, some people within the church hierarchy opposed the change and it definitely was not welcomed by the elite. They often regarded it as sinister, or verging on "communistic."

Religions of El Salvador (1995)	
Roman Catholic	78%
Protestant	17%
Other Christians	2%
Other	3%

Archbishop Oscar Romero

Archbishop Oscar Romero was a Salvadoran from the small town of Ciudad Barrios in northeastern Honduras. Born in 1917, he left school at age twelve and began work as a carpenter. Soon he decided to become a Catholic priest. He began his training in the nearby city of San Miguel and completed his studies in Rome. When Romero returned to El Salvador, he became well known for his weekly radio sermons. In 1977, he was appointed archbishop of San Salvador, and during the next three years, he tried to use his influence to calm the tense political situation. But the oppression seemed without end: "We suffer with those who have disappeared, those who have had to flee their homes, and those who have been tortured." His voice was heard, and he was seen as a threat by the wealthy, powerful elite.

In February 1980, he wrote to U.S. president Jimmy Carter, asking him to stop sending U.S. aid to the military in El Salvador. During a sermon on March 23, he turned to the soldiers and begged them to stop the repression. The next day, as he was delivering Mass in the chapel of the Hospital of Divine Providence, Archbishop Romero was murdered by a bullet from one of the notorious death squads.

At his funeral a week later (below), the crowds were fearful, but somber and defiant. Political banners were everywhere. As the procession with the coffin began, rifle fire opened up, and many people were killed. Many of the wounded were shot as they tried to crawl into the cathedral.

In El Salvador, however, there was a tremendous desire for change. Small groups of people who worshiped together discussed their problems and even planned some protest actions. The spirit of change moved as quickly as the tensions within Salvadoran society. As the priests saw the conflict spreading, they began to speak out for compassion and call for an end to the oppression of the poor. Some clergy took the side of the poor. Some were killed because their ideas were not acceptable to the powerful and wealthy elite and the military.

Protestant Churches

While the Catholic Church sought a new, liberal position between the wealthy ruling elite and the masses of poor people, the strength of the Protestant churches increased. The Protestant influence was small until the 1950s—a handful of missionaries of the Central American Mission, a Quaker group, some Seventh-Day Adventists, and a few Baptists working in the towns. The balance changed rapidly in the second half of the twentieth century, however, especially after 1978. More faiths and money poured in from the United States. The political turmoil left most Salvadorans bewildered, needing to rely on strong family ties and hope for a better future.

The media, which had been used to powerful effect by Archbishop Oscar Romero, have become the route to the hearts of the people. Radio stations send spiritual messages from almost 100 evangelical groups.

A Protestant baptism in Lake Coatepeque

A Family Affair

Building a community church is a family affair for the people of a run-down street in southern San Salvador. They are members of one of the many evangelical Protestant churches that have found willing followers among the poor of this sprawling city. Money to buy building materials comes from the United States, gathered by devout people who believe a better way of life should be available to all who trust in the teachings of Jesus Christ. Their message is carried across the globe on the Internet.

For the street people, the day begins with simple food—also donated—and they pray together as a community to give thanks. Some then write cards to send to the donors, while others mend clothes or sort rubbish. The church is built with willing hands working under the guidance of the pastor. The new strength the people gain by working together helps them through the days in which a paid job is still a distant dream.

New churches, often simple one-story buildings, have been built, some in the poorest shantytowns. Satellite television carries powerful messages from the United States, and well-known U.S. evangelists have drawn crowds that filled stadiums. Outside relief agencies use the evangelical network to send food and medicine to distant parts of the country, and small meetinghouses and education programs have blossomed.

Arts and
Crafts

C ULTURE, THE ARTS, SPORTS, AND LEISURE HAVE ALL been severely disrupted by El Salvador's turbulent history, government repression, and civil war. But even before the Chapultepec Peace Accords were announced in 1992, a small cultural revolution was taking place. Publishers, writers, artists, and musical groups were beginning to emerge from the shadows. They used their art to express their feelings about the violence and carnage that had torn apart their lives and their country. Now, as they enter the twenty-first century, there is a feeling that it is time for Salvadorans to look beyond the war and its consequences.

Opposite: **An ancient Mayan ceramic jug**

Handicrafts

The Maya and other native peoples produced fine artifacts of ceramic and stone, massive stone buildings, musical instruments made of reed and wood, and jewelry of semiprecious stones and gold. Salvadorans today have maintained the tradition, and craftspeople still make handicrafts in many parts of the country.

A Museum of Words and Images

The new *Museo de la Palabra y la Imagen* (Museum of Words and Images) is collecting film and video footage, photographs, historical books, and manuscripts on El Salvador. The collection will be used to create a common background from which future generations can develop their own ideas. People have been asked to search their attics and old trunks, and much interesting material has been found. The goal is to record the evolution of El Salvador, beginning with ancient artifacts left by the first inhabitants. The museum is still in its infancy, but it already travels the country with a mobile exhibit.

Rows of intricately painted toys

Some of the most recognizable crafts are the colorful geometric designs from La Palma, a small town in the mountains north of San Salvador. Salvadoran artist Fernando Llort taught these designs to the villagers by in 1970. Today, they are painted on wood, leather, and ceramics in more than 100 small workshops. Toys and other handicrafts are also decorated with brightly colored images of people, villages, and farming life.

Artists in the town of Ilobasco, northeast of San Salvador, produce ornaments made of ceramic and clay, including *sorpresas* (surprises)—small oval shells with tiny clay figures, nativity

Tiny clay figures known as "surprises"

scenes, and depictions of village life hidden inside. San Sebastián, also close to San Salvador, is known for its hand-loomed textiles. Hammocks, bedspreads, and tablecloths with matching napkins are among the most popular items. Here, most of the weaving is done by the men, a tradition passed down for generations. The women finish the items and sell them in the small shops that line the streets of the town. Inside the houses stand large, handmade looms and stone vessels in which cotton threads are hand-dyed. The threads are then hung on bamboo rods and dried in the sun.

In eastern El Salvador, people spin plant fibers into twine that is used to make rope and hammocks. Handmade rattan furniture is crafted in the south.

A worker weaving textiles in San Sebastián

The National Theater

The National Theater is one of the grandest buildings in San Salvador. It was built in the early twentieth century in a Renaissance style that reflects the influence of French culture. The interior has been restored to look as it did in the old days, with plush red-velvet furnishings; marble pillars; gold-leaf trimmings; chandeliers from Austria; scrolled, decorative plaster-work; and fine paintings. A 2,500-square-foot (232-sq-m) mural covers the ceiling. Cultural activities staged there range from new and old plays and concerts of classical music to modern Latin American protest music.

Music

Some instruments similar to those used by the Indians hundreds of years ago are still popular today. They include pipes made from wood or reed, drums, whistles, and wooden *marimbas*, which resemble xylophones. Together with Andean panpipes and flutes from the highlands of Peru, Bolivia, and Ecuador, these instruments are part of the folk music scene in El Salvador. Known as *canción popular*, folk music is both traditional and contemporary. Music festivals include folk singers with guitars and percussion instruments who sing about things that are happening in the country today. Folk music has influenced some classical Salvadoran musicians, particularly María Mendoza de Baratta, a leading twentieth-century composer.

Celebrating a Special Birthday

Girls all over El Salvador celebrate their fifteenth birthday to mark the beginning of womanhood. The celebration depends on the family's circumstances, and it includes grand parties for the daughters of wealthy families. Girls from modest or working families sometimes celebrate in a corner of the sprawling craft markets near the cathedral in Plaza Barrios in downtown San Salvador. A shrine stands in one corner of the market, and balloons and paper chains decorate the roof. Friends and family, all dress up, including children, and a small group of musicians take their place at one side. In one corner, a table is piled with presents. The birthday girl sits with the guests to listen to readings by a minister, and everyone stands to join in the singing. The ceremony is primarily religious, and stallholders and passersby in the market are invited to join in the celebrations.

The influence of Mexican mural art is evident in this painting.

Artists

Before the twentieth century, paintings in El Salvador consisted mainly of portraits or religious themes. But when artists began traveling in Europe and elsewhere early in the 1900s, they returned to El Salvador with new ideas. Some were influenced by impressionism, for instance, while others studied mural art in Mexico. One of these painters was Carlos Alberto Imery (1879–1949), who founded El Salvador's first school of art. A second art school was founded in 1935 by Valero Lecha (1894–1976), a Spanish painter who was responsible for training many of the twentieth century's leading artists.

Among Valero Lecha's students was Rosa Mena Valenzuela (born in 1924), known for her bold brush strokes, vibrant colors, and mystical subjects, and Julia Díaz (born 1917) who studied overseas before returning to El Salvador. Díaz became an admired portrait artist and a painter of mothers and children. In 1973, Valenzuela founded the Academy of Painting and Drawing that carries her name. Díaz founded the Museo Forma, the only museum of twentieth-century painting and sculpture in the country. Another important figure in the move to modern art was Spanish-trained Carlos Cañas (born 1924). Others include Noé Canjura and Elas Reyes.

Internationally, El Salvador's most acclaimed artist is probably Benjamin Canas (1933–1987). He has been called the most important painter of the "fantastic" in Latin America. His paintings show human beings mixed with mythological, historical, or religious figures. Fernando Llort and Alfredo Linares are two of El Salvador's best-known contemporary painters, known for the gaiety and color that dominate their work. Linares, like Llort, comes from the mountainous region of Chalatenango. In many of his paintings, he too uses bold, solid colors to represent anonymous people, town, villages, landscapes and natural features. Another notable contemporary painter is César Menéndez (born 1954), whose work often has a social or political significance. Some of his paintings show the tragedies and evils of the civil war, such as *The Party at the Well*, which portrays death after a massacre.

Salarrué

Novelist, sculptor, painter, and poet, Salvador Efrain Salazar Arrue—affectionately known as Salarrué—was El Salvador's most versatile artist. He was born on October 22, 1899, in Sonsonate.

Salarrué began his career as a novelist, with *The Black Christ*. He went on to achieve international acclaim with a book of short stories, *Tales of Mud* (1933), some of which have become Salvadoran classics. Much of their appeal is in the magic and superstition that Salarrué weaves into his stories. In 1945, he produced a highly original collection called *Kids' Stories*, which sought to imitate the way Salvadoran urchins talk among themselves.

Fantasy was also an important theme in Salarrué's paintings, as seen in the weird and wonderful designs with which he illustrated *O'yarkandal* (1929). Many of his later compositions retain that sense of mystery. Salurrue died in 1975, a year after his wife, Zelie, who was also an artist. Today, their daughter Maya is a leading Salvadoran artist.

El Salvador has produced few novelists, but many poets. Poetry was the favored literary form in El Salvador throughout the twentieth century, though there also have been important works by writers of short stories and essays.

Francisco Gavidia, a poet, essayist, translator, dramatist, and playwright, is considered the first major figure of Salvadoran literature. Born in December 1863, he witnessed much of his nation's painful history before he died, aged 92, in 1955. He was a man of his time, as comfortable with translations of ancient Greek myth and legend as with the lives of contemporary Central American heroes. In *Stories and Tales*, he blends personal memories with national history. His poem *To Central America* portrays a strong desire for the unity of Central America, combined with a hatred of tyranny and a faith in democracy.

Alfredo Espino is regarded by many as El Salvador's national poet. He died in 1928 aged only twenty-eight. The poems in *Cups of Sadness* published after his death, are filled with a love and passion for his country, and are revered by Salvadoran exiles.

Claudia Lars (whose real name was Carmen Brannon) lived from 1899 to 1974. She is considered El Salvador's leading female poet. Her best-known early works include *Stars in the Well*, while later in life she produced *Our Pulsating World* (1969), which attempts to put her country in perspective against events such as the conquest of space and the arrival of the Beatles.

While most artists and writers have been affected by political events in El Salvador, few were more committed to the revolutionary struggle than Roque Dalton. Born into a wealthy family, he campaigned against social injustice. He was arrested and sentenced to death. He wrote some of his best-known works while in exile between 1960 and 1973, including his collection of poems *In a Tavern and Other Places* and *What a Dud Poet I Was!* When Dalton returned from exile, he joined the guerrilla forces, but they accused him of spying and executed him in 1975.

El Salvador's best-known contemporary writers are Claribel Alegría (born 1924) and Manlio Argueta (born 1935). Alegría has written many collections of poetry and is also a novelist. She writes about the effects of the civil war on peasants and women. Her novel *Ashes of Izalco* won her much acclaim. Argueta lived in exile until recently. He, too, writes of the tragedy and destruction of the war, most notably in his novel *One Day of Life*.

The civil war of the 1980s produced another generation of writers tormented by the horrors of what was happening to their country. Foremost among them is David Escobar Galindo (born 1943), a poet and novelist whose titles include *Ceremonial Wake for Violence* and *Lament for Violence*. However, he has also written a series of popular short stories about daily life in El Salvador's towns and villages for *La Prensa Gráfica*, the leading Salvadoran daily newspaper. They suggest a shift from the dark days of the war into a new, more optimistic era.

Sports and Leisure

Few but the wealthy can enjoy organized club sports in El Salvador, but most Salvadorans are passionate about soccer. Children kick balls around the streets or on any open land, and in most towns there are stadiums for regular matches.

Young children learn to play soccer.

A soccer game between
Honduras and El Salvador

Countrywide, everyone follows major competitions such as the World Cup qualifiers. World Cup qualifying matches took place in Central America between July and November 2000. The teams taking part in Group D were El Salvador, Honduras, Jamaica, and the West Indian state of Saint Vincent and the Grenadines. Baseball, volleyball, and basketball are also popular.

For many families, time off means a trip to the beach to swim, to relax in the sun, or to surf. There are also many beautiful, scenic areas in the countryside—including some of the national parks—where people walk and picnic.

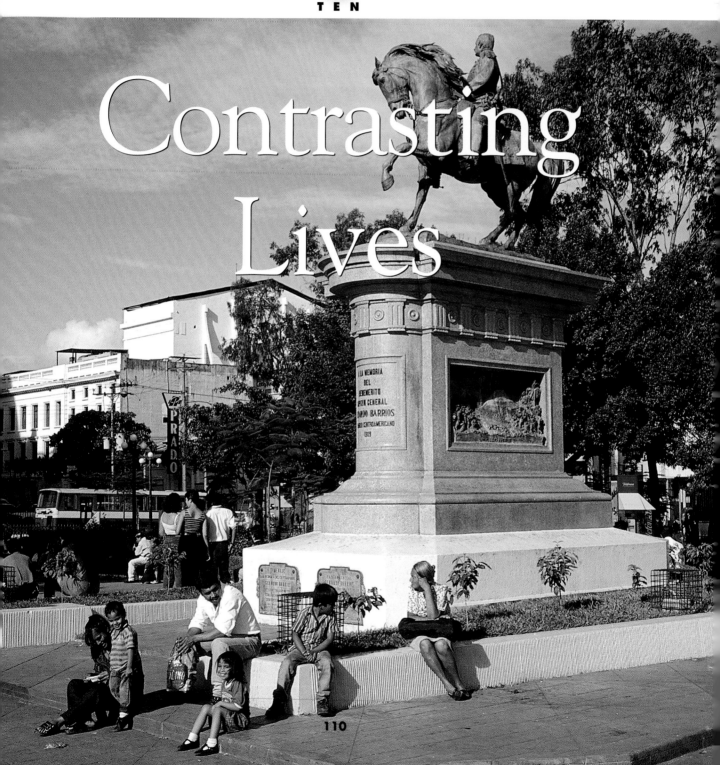

Contrasting Lives

B ECAUSE A FEW WEALTHY POWERFUL FAMILIES HAVE controlled El Salvador for centuries, there is a wide gap between the rich and the poor. Little attention has been paid to most of the population. Poverty is widespread, and the standard of living is very low. As a result, many rural families move to the cities and towns hoping to find a better life. It seldom happens. Although jobs and health and education facilities are generally more available in the cities, there are not enough of them to serve the large numbers of people arriving each day.

Home and Family

Housing is a problem for many Salvadorans. While the wealthy live in quiet residential suburbs, in large houses with

House of a wealthy family in a suburb

gardens, swimming pools, garages, and sophisticated alarm systems, the poor go without the basic necessities of sanitation, electricity, and running water. Most live on the outskirts of the cities and towns in shantytowns called *tugurios*. Their homes are made of tin or cardboard, with dirt floors and makeshift furniture. Others live in overcrowded conditions in run-down city buildings with poor sanitation and no washing or cooking facilities. Between these extremes, the small Salvadoran middle class rent or own modest apartments, or live in small suburban houses.

In shanytowns many homes are made of tin and cardboard.

In the countryside, a typical house—called a *choza*—is built of adobe mud bricks or of woven sticks covered in mud, with tile or tin roofing. Several generations often live together in one small house, using curtains to separate sleeping and living quarters. Cooking is usually done outside on a wood or charcoal fire. There is no electricity. Candles and kerosene lamps provide light indoors. Water has to be carried from the nearest stream or river.

An adobe house in the country

National Holidays in El Salvador

New Year's Day	January 1
Labor Day	May 1
Independence Day	September 15
Columbus Day	October 12
Anniversary of the First Call for Independence	November 5

Much of this work is done by women. In addition to caring for the family and keeping the home clean, they may walk or ride several miles to wash clothes in the river or to buy food. Women also tend the family vegetable plot and raise pigs or chickens in the backyard. They may sell extra produce or small handicrafts in the market. Men are employed on the plantations and by the local landowner—when there is work.

The family is the heart of Salvadoran life, despite the extreme circumstances that have divided so many of them. Few families have not been affected by the civil war.

Salvadoran parents usually have several children.

Salvadoran families are large, with an average of four children. Rural women often have more than twice that number of children, however. For most, this high birthrate is an economic necessity because children can work and earn money. It is also due to Roman Catholic teachings against contraception and abortion. The government has actively supported birth-control programs, however.

Families are also made larger by the "extended" family, which includes godparents, who are expected to help look after their godchildren. Salvadorans, despite all their hardships, are warm, outgoing, hospitable, and friendly people. If any member of the family needs a helping hand, someone will provide it.

Going to School

Very few Salvadoran children get the education they need, and the illiteracy rate is high. More than one-fourth of people over age fifteen are unable to read and write. About 55 percent of rural women are illiterate. Education standards were poor before the war, and ten years of fighting totally disrupted whatever facilities existed. Although the postwar governments have promised to improve standards, progress has been painfully slow. In fact, the percentage of the national budget devoted to education actually dropped from 17 percent in 1990 to 15 percent in 1995.

Officially, there are four levels of education in El Salvador. Preschool, for children ages four to five, is followed by nine years of primary school. Then come secondary school, for grades 10 through 12, and higher education. The vast majority

Children attending primary school

of students—about 80 percent—start at primary level, but less than one-third move on to secondary school.

The principal reasons why students fail to attend school or drop out are cost, the family's need to put children to work, and the lack of schools, particularly in rural areas. Although public schools are free, books, equipment, uniforms, and registration have to be paid for, and many families cannot afford them.

Private schools generally offer a higher standard of learning than public schools and have better facilities. But private schools and universities are available only to students who can afford them, and most cannot . The two foremost universities are the University of Central America and the National University. The University of Central America is considered academically superior, and it attracts wealthier students. The facilities and standards of the National University suffered from its association with left-wing soldiers during the civil war.

Entrance to the University of Central America

During the war, schools all but disappeared in several parts of the country. To counter this situation, an alternative education system developed, known as "popular education." It relies on volunteer teachers, usually members of local communities and returning refugees. Often, the teachers themselves have no more than a third-grade education. Working in makeshift buildings and with little equipment, they have managed to create some degree of formal education, which rural children otherwise would not get. Subjects include history, geography, physical education, and mathematics. Today, the position of the popular education teachers is unclear. The government would prefer to control all education, but it needs their help.

Games

Whoever has the *mica* is "it." The mica is imaginary, and players try to pass it on. It is kind of like playing tag. Whoever is "it" decides where to pass the mica—to the ear, the shoulder, the hand, or the leg.

Salvadoran children also play games like *peregrina*, *chibola*, and *capirucho*, which are similar to hopscotch, marbles, and yo-yos. Another game is *trompo*. Learning how to spin the *trompo*, a wooden top, takes skill and practice.

Benjamin Bloom Hospital in San Salvador is El Salvador's largest public hospital.

Health

Health services in El Salvador are woefully inadequate for all but the wealthy few who can afford private treatment. There are not enough hospitals, clinics, doctors, beds, equipment, or medicine to go around. Waiting lists in the main hospitals in San Salvador are very long—months for even major surgery. Unsanitary conditions inside some hospitals increase the risks of having an operation.

In 1996, statistics gathered by the United Nations showed high infant and child mortality rates. Many of these deaths were caused by illnesses such as diarrhea, and by respiratory problems that often are curable. On average, there was only 1 doctor for every 1,563 people. Only 43 percent of the population had access to safe drinking water.

This man sells herbal remedies.

During the civil war, government-provided health facilities disappeared from many rural areas. Private organizations stepped in and did their best to provide basic services. They trained local people to become health workers and were effective in saving many lives. Even so, at the end of the war only 20 percent of the rural population had direct access to health services.

Many people have no choice but to use age-old remedies or visit *curanderos* (herbal doctors). However, they often have more faith in these traditional healing methods than in modern medicine. Bags and boxes of herbs are sold in most markets for ailments ranging from headaches and upset stomachs to insomnia and depression. Curanderos also use these herbs with their own special powders and rituals.

Water Pollution

Heavy agriculture and a high population density bring many problems. For El Salvador, serious water pollution is just one of them. Less than one-third of the population has proper sewage disposal; drains often lead to streams. In some areas, sewage also pollutes community wells (below). Added to the human waste are chemical fertilizers and pesticides. Industrial waste products and garbage are simply tossed in the countryside. The effects of these actions are that 90 percent of El Salvador's water resources are contaminated. Many illnesses and birth defects are reported each year.

Typical Foods

The most common foods in El Salvador are rice, beans, and tortillas, which women make fresh every day. In poor homes and rural areas, this is the staple diet, with little variation except, perhaps, some vegetables, soups, and occasionally meat. This diet is filling and sustains families for hard work in the fields, but it is deficient in protein and vitamins and leads to serious nutritional problems over time.

This woman makes and sells tortillas on the street.

In towns and cities, people have more choice if they can afford variety. Markets are filled with fresh fruit and vegetables of every kind as well as chickens, turkey, and a wide range of fish. Some restaurants specialize in local fish, including shrimp, lobster, and swordfish. A favorite dish is *ceviche*—raw fish marinated in lemon or lime juice. Another traditional food is *panes con pavo*—rolls filled with turkey and served with salad. At fiesta times, especially, women make *tamales*—cornmeal dough filled with meat or chicken and boiled in a leaf.

Relatively new but growing rapidly in most towns are fast-food restaurants serving U.S.- and Mexican-style snacks and drinks. They are especially popular with young people and with city and town workers who cannot get home for lunch. Traditionally, lunch, or *almuerzo*, is the main meal in El Salvador, but many city workers now find it more convenient to eat their main meal in the evening with their families.

A Salvadoran Specialty

From an early age, Salvadoran girls learn to make *pupusas*, the national snack, which is unique to El Salvador. Pupusas are small, thick corn tortillas filled with cheese, beans, meat, or sausage. They are delicious eaten directly from the griddle where they are cooked. They are served with *cortido*, a mixture of shredded green cabbage, onion, carrots, and garlic. You can buy pupusas anywhere in El Salvador, from *pupuserias*. These can be anything from homemade street-side griddles to small roadside stores to large, barnlike buildings that are crowded with families on weekends.

A woman buys a newspaper at a newsstand.

Five daily newspapers are published in San Salvador, and Santa Ana and San Miguel each has its own daily paper. The two largest papers—*La Prensa Gráfica*, established in 1915, and *El Diario de Hoy*, founded in 1936—are both connected to wealthy, influential families. They take the conservative point of view. At the other political extreme is *Diario Latino*, El Salvador's oldest paper, founded in 1892. The two remaining dailies are *El Mundo* and *La Noticia*. They are more moderate in their views and less influential.

Since the civil war, all the papers have had to modify or alter their viewpoint. Peace has brought a desire for less political journalism, and the papers have had to embrace new technology and accept advertising to help pay their way. High-quality color is essential as are articles on international and regional affairs and good coverage of arts and sports. Important periodicals include *Orientación*, the official newspaper of the Roman Catholic Church, and *Proceso*, a well-written weekly news journal published by the University of Central America.

In the last two decades, television has grown more than any other form of media. Today, it plays a significant part in the political and educational life of the people. During the 1980s, one channel produced some of the best news coverage in Central America and surprised its audiences by conducting interviews between some of the main adversaries in the war. Programs from other parts of the Americas are also shown, including movies, sports coverage, CNN, and *CNN en Español*.

Many people listen to radio shows, especially in rural communities. The Catholic Church has its own station, and other channels are devoted to educational programs and women's issues.

Offices of a TV station in El Salvador

Rebel Radio

From the beginning of the civil war, the guerrillas knew they needed their own radio stations to get their message to the people, especially in rural areas. In much secrecy, the rebels created two stations—Radio Venceremos and Radio Farabundo Martí.

Radio Venceremos first broadcast in 1979. The guerrillas painted graffiti on walls urging people to tune in, and they passed out leaflets advertising the "People's Revolutionary Radio." By early 1980, they were transmitting from the National University, always on the lookout in case they or their aerials were detected. They did not stay in one place long because it was too dangerous. And that became the pattern of the media during the war. Always in danger, sometimes under attack from gunfire or helicopters, battling high-tech jamming as the government tried to stop them, the rebel radio stations were continually on the run. However, they lasted all through the war, and afterward, both stations were given legal status.

The Future

The 1992 peace accords gave Salvadorans hope that their future would be different—and better. Perhaps the greatest achievements have been peace itself, and the presence of political parties in a democratic system that represents all the people. The economy has also grown stronger. But so far, there has been little improvement in the daily lives of most Salvadorans, and little indication of change among the few wealthy families that still have too large a voice in running the country. A sinister and unwelcome development has been a soaring rise in crime. In 1995, a survey found that 60 percent of Salvadorans reported that they or a family member had been the victim of a violent crime.

Peace has given El Salvador an opportunity to address some of its fundamental problems. As we enter this new millennium, we must hope that the Salvadoran government will seize the chance to give future generations a better chance and a more just society.

People celebrate peace in
El Salvador.

Timeline

El Salvador's History	
Maya people arrive in El Salvador from Mexico.	1200 B.C.
Mayan civilization reaches its peak.	A.D. 300–900
Mayan civilization collapses; Pipil people settle along the Pacific coast.	Late 900s
Spanish arrive but are resisted by the Pipil.	1524
Pedro de Alvarado founds San Salvador; the Pipil force the Spanish to withdraw.	1525
Spanish establish control over El Salvador.	1528–1540
Fewer than 10,000 Indians remain in El Salvador.	1600
Father José Matías Delgado leads El Salvador's first call for independence from Spain.	1811
United Provinces of Central America is formed.	1823
Manuel José Arce of El Salvador becomes president of the United Provinces.	1825
San Salvador becomes capital of the United Provinces.	1834
United Provinces of Central America is dissolved.	1838
El Salvador adopts a constitution and becomes an independent republic.	1841

World History	
2500 B.C.	Egyptians build the Pyramids and Sphinx in Giza.
563 B.C.	Buddha is born in India.
A.D. 313	The Roman emperor Constantine recognizes Christianity.
610	The prophet Muhammad begins preaching a new religion called Islam.
1054	The Eastern (Orthodox) and Western (Roman) Churches break apart.
1066	William the Conqueror defeats the English in the Battle of Hastings.
1095	Pope Urban II proclaims the First Crusade.
1215	King John seals the Magna Carta.
1300s	The Renaissance begins in Italy.
1347	The Black Death sweeps through Europe.
1453	Ottoman Turks capture Constantinople, conquering the Byzantine Empire.
1492	Columbus arrives in North America.
1500s	The Reformation leads to the birth of Protestantism.
1776	The Declaration of Independence is signed.
1789	The French Revolution begins.

El Salvador's History

El Salvador experiences unstable governments at home and wars with neighboring countries.	1841–1876
The government passes laws that take communal lands away from Indians.	1882
General Maximiliano Hernández Martínez takes control of the government and rules as a dictator.	1931
Martínez crushes a revolt by farmworkers and executes 10,000 people.	1932
Student and soldier revolutionaries overthrow Martínez.	1944
President Oscar Osorio begins reform projects.	1950
Military coups bring Julio Adalberto Tivera to power.	1960–1961
National Conciliation Party controls the government.	1961–1979
"Soccer War" between El Salvador and Honduras.	1969
Protesters demand jobs and land for the poor.	Late 1970s
General Carlos Humberto Romero becomes president.	1977
Army officers replace Romero; civil war breaks out.	1979
Archbishop Oscar Arnulfo Romero is assassinated; José Napoleón Duarte becomes president; Honduras and El Salvador sign a peace treaty.	1980
Civil war begins; U.S. supports El Salvador's government.	1980s
A new Constitution restores democracy.	1983
José Napoleón Duarte is elected president.	1984
Earthquake hits San Salvador, killing more than 1,000 people.	1986
A peace treaty ends the civil war.	1992
Armando Calderón Sol is elected president.	1994
Francisco Flores is elected president.	1999
Earthquakes near San Salvador kill more than 1,000 people.	2001

World History

1865	The American Civil War ends.
1914	World War I breaks out.
1917	The Bolshevik Revolution brings Communism to Russia.
1929	Worldwide economic depression begins.
1939	World War II begins, following the German invasion of Poland.
1945	World War II ends.
1957	The Vietnam War starts.
1969	Humans land on the moon.
1975	The Vietnam War ends.
1979	Soviet Union invades Afghanistan.
1983	Drought and famine in Africa.
1989	The Berlin Wall is torn down, as Communism crumbles in Eastern Europe.
1991	Soviet Union breaks into separate states.
1992	Bill Clinton is elected U.S. president.
2000	George W. Bush is elected U.S. president.

Fast Facts

Official name: Republic of El Salvador

Capital: San Salvador

Official language: Spanish

San Salvador

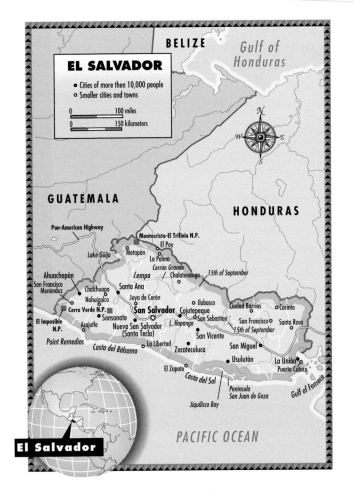

El Salvador's flag

Harvesting watermelons

Official religion:	None
Founding date:	1841
National anthem:	*"Saludemos la patria orgullosos"* ("We Proudly Salute the Fatherland")
Government:	Republic
Chief of state:	President
Head of government:	President
Area:	8,124 square miles (21,040 sq km)
Dimensions:	East-west, 163 miles (262 km); north-south, 88 miles (142 km)
Latitude and longitude of geographic center:	13° 50' North, 88° 55' West
Borders:	Guatemala to the west; Honduras to the north and east; the Pacific Ocean to the south
Highest elevation:	Cerro El Pital, 8,957 feet (2,730 m) above sea level
Lowest elevation:	Sea level along the Pacific Ocean
Average temperature extremes:	In January, 60°F (16°C), in San Salvador; in March, 94°F (34°C) in San Salvador
Average precipitation extremes:	85 inches (216 cm) along the coast; 60 inches (150 cm) in the northwest
National population (2000 est.):	6,122,515

Montecristo National Park

Currency

Population of largest cities (1995 est):

San Salvador	422,570
Santa Ana	202,337
San Miguel	182,817
Nueva San Salvador	116,575
Ahuachapán	83,885

Famous landmarks:
- ▶ *Caves of Espiritu Santo* and *Cabeza de Duende*
- ▶ *Cerro Verde National Park*
- ▶ *Los Chorros waterfall*
- ▶ *Costa del Sol* and *Costa del Bálsamo beaches*
- ▶ *El Imposible National Park*
- ▶ *Jardin Botánico La Laguna*
- ▶ *Montecristo National Park*
- ▶ *Tazumal archaeological site* in Chalchuapa

Industry: El Salvador's government encourages the growth of industry, and manufacturing is a significant part of the economy. Major industries include food-and-beverage processing, oil refining, textile and shoe manufacturing, and the production of cigarettes and chemicals. Limestone is the country's largest mining product.

Currency: El Salvador's traditional currency was the colón; U.S.$1 = 8.76 colones in 2001. In January 2001, the U.S. dollar was declared El Salvador's national currency.

System of weights and measures: The metric system is the standard; other units are also used, such as the *libra* (1.014 pounds or 0.46 kg) and the *quintal* (100 pounds or 45.36 kg).

Literacy (1990 est.): 71 percent

Schoolchildren

Common Spanish words and phrases:

Adiós.	Good-bye.
almuerzo	lunch
Buenos días.	Good morning.
Buenas noches.	Good evening/Good night.
campesino	a person who lives in the countryside; a peasant
canción popular	folk music
¿Cómo estás?	How are you?
curandero	herbal doctor
¿Dónde está . . .?	Where is . . . ?
Gracias.	Thank you.
hacienda	large farm
¡Hola!	Hello.
mestizos	people of mixed Spanish and Indian ancestry
no	no
por favor	please
pupusas	small, filled tortillas
sí	yes
tugurios	shanty towns

Famous people:

Anastasio Aquino (1800s)
Rebel leader

José Napoleón Duarte (1925–1990)
Politician

Alfredo Espino (1900?–1928)
Poet

Agustín Farabundo Martí (?–1932)
Student political leader

Claudia Lars (Carmen Brannon) (1899–1974)
Poet

José Matías Delgado (1767–?)
Priest and politician

Archbishop Oscar Romero (1917–1980)
Religious leader and activist

Salarrué (Salvador Efrain Salazar Arrue) (1899–1975)
Artist and writer

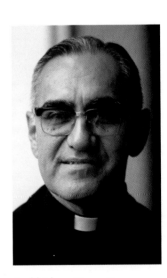

Archbishop Oscar Romero

To Find Out More

Nonfiction

▶ Dalton, Roque. *Small Hours of the Night: Selected Poems of Roque Dalton*. Willimantic, Conn.: Curbstone Press, 1996.

▶ Foley, Erin. *World Cultures: El Salvador*. Tarrytown, NY: Marshall Cavendish, 1995.

▶ López Vigil, José Ignacio. *Rebel Radio*. Willimantic, Conn.: Curbstone Press, 1994.

▶ Macdonald, Mandy, and Mike Gatehouse. *In the Mountains of Morazan*. London: Latin American Bureau, 1995.

▶ Murray, Kevin. *El Salvador, Peace on Trial*. An Oxfam Country Profile. Oxford, England: Oxfam Publications, 1997.

▶ Murray, Kevin, and Tom Barry. *Inside El Salvador*. Albuquerque, N.M.: Interhemispheric Resource Center, 1995.

▶ Sanders, Renfield. *Major World Nations: El Salvador*. Broomall, PA: Chelsea House, 1997.

Websites

▶ **El Salvador on the Web**
www.lanic.utexas.edu/la/ca/Salvador
*Contains many sections on all aspects
of El Salvador.*

▶ **El Diario de Hoy**
www.elsalvador.com/noticias/
index.html
*Daily newspaper from El Salvador,
in Spanish.*

▶ **Maps of El Salvador**
www.infoplease.com/atlas/country/
elsalvador.html
*Displays maps plus fast facts about
El Salvador.*

▶ **Salvadoran Recipes**
http://latinoculture.about.com/
culture/latinoculture/os/
salvadoranrecipes
Gives links to many recipes.

Organizations and Embassies

▶ **Embassy of El Salvador**
2308 California Street N.W.
Washington, D.C. 20008
(202) 265-9671

Index

Page numbers in *italics* indicate illustrations.

A

Aberle, Juan, 67
agriculture, 71–74. *See also* farming
Ahuachapán, 23
Alegría, Claribel, 107
Alvarado, Pedro de, 40, *40*, 66
ancient Mayan ceramic jug, *99*
Aquino, Anastasio, 44
Araujo, Arturo, 46
Arce, Manuel José, 43, *43*
archaeological site, *39*
ARENA, 52, 54, 59, 60–61
Argueta, Manlio, 107
Army of Liberation, 44
Arrieta, Roberto D'Aubuisson, 52, 54, *54*, 58
Arrue, Salvador Efrain Salazar, 105
artists, 104–105
astronomy, 93
Atlacatl Battalion, 58

B

balsam (trees), 75, *75*
Baratta, María Mendoza de, 103
Benjamin Bloom Hospital, *119*
birthday celebrations, 103, *103*
Bonaparte, Joseph, 43
borders, 15
Bosque, Pio Romero, 46
Brannon, Carmen, 106
Burkard, Alfredo Cristiani, 54, 69
Burnt Islands, 19

C

cacao (chocolate), 39, 41
Canas, Benjamin, 105
Cañas, Carlos, 105
Canas, Juan José, 67
Canjura, Noé, 105
Castro, Fidel, 50
Catholic women killed by military, *52*
caves, 21
celebration of peace, *127*
Central American Common Market, 74
Central American Federation, 10
Cerro El Pital, 15
ceviche (food), 123
Chapultepec Peace Accords, 55–57, 81
children playing, *90*, *118*
children playing soccer, *108*
choza, 113
Christian Democratic Party (PDC), 49
city park, *110*
civil war, 13, 35, 51–55, 76
civil war memorial, *13*
clay figure "surprises," *100*
climate, 25
Clinton, Bill, *70*
coastline, 22, 24
coffee, 23, 45–46, 72
coffee factory workers, *48*
Cojutepeque shrine, 94, *94*
colibri, *26*
Colomoncagua camp, 89
Columbus, Christopher, 76

Communist Party, 50
community well, *121*
conservation, 27–28, 30–31, 34–35
Constitution, 54, 63
continental drift, 17
Cortés, Hernan, 40
cost of living, 78
Costa del Bálsamo, 24
cotton, 72
country adobe house, *113*
crafts, 99–101
crime, 126
crops. *See* farming
Cuidad Segundo Montes, 90–91
culture, 99–101
curanderos, 120–121
currency, 76, *76*

D

Dalton, Roque, 107
dam on the Río Lempa, *78*
death squads, 50, 58, 59
Delgado, José Matías, 43
Democratic Convergence (CD) party, 59
Díaz, Julia, 104–105
domestic violence, 87
Duarte, José Napoleón, 49, 51, 54, 64, *64*

E

earthquakes, 9, 13, 17–20
economy, 24
    by wealthy elite, 47–48, 80–81
    dollar revenue, 76–77
    effects of Great Depression, 46
    financial aid and rescue plan, 69–81
    and high birthrate, 115
    and land reform, 57
    under new democracy, 126
ecosystem, 32
education, 46, 88, 115–118
egret, *31*

El Mozote, 53, *53*, 58
election fraud, 49, 50
election posters, *59*
elections, 59
emigration, 76
employment, 71, 73, 75, 85–86, *87*, 114
encomienda system, 41–42
Espino, Alfredo, 106

F

family, 113–115
family harvesting watermelons, *68*
farming, 10, 23, 27, 71–74. *See also* coffee
    Mayan, 37–38
    Pipil, 39
farmland in Los Naranjos, *11*
Fátima, 94
FDR, 52–53, 54
female office worker, *88*
FMLN, 50–51, 52, 54–56, 58, 59–61
folk music, 103
foods, 122–123
forestry, 74
Fourteen Families, 41
Free Zone industry, 75
Frente Faribundo Martí de Liberación
    Nacional. *See* FMLN
funeral of Oscar Romero, *95*

G

Galindo, David Escobar, 107
games, 118
gar fish, 32
Gavidia, Francisco, 106
geography, 15–24
geothermal power, 23
Gondwanaland, 17
government, 63–65, 67
    military rule, 47–50
    political parties, 67

Government of National Unity, 54
Great Depression, 46
Gulf of Fonseca, *34*, 34–35

H
handicrafts, 99–101
health care services, 119–121
henequen, 21
herbal medicine, 120–121
hieroglyphics, 38
holidays
    national, 114
    religious, 94
holy week procession, *93*
hot mineral springs, 23
house of a wealthy family, *111*
housing, 111–113
human rights, 57–59
hydroelectric power, 24, 77–78

I
Imery, Carlos Alberto, 104
immigration, 49, 76
independence, 42–44
indigo, 41
Iturbide, Agustín de, 43
Izalco Volcano, 19, *19*

J
Joya de Cerén, 9–10

L
La Matanza, 46–47
Ladinos, 84–86
lagoons, 25, 31–33
Laguna Caldera Volcano, 9
Laguna El Jocotal *33*
Lake Illopango, *18*, 18–19
land reform, 57, 80–81
Land Reform Law, 81

languages
    Nahuatl, 38, 83, 86
    popular expressions, 89
    Spanish, 86
Lars, Claudia, 106
Laurasia, 17
Lecha, Valero, 104
Legislative Assembly building, *64*
Lighthouse of the Pacific, 19, *19*
Linares, Alfredo, 105
literacy, 115–118
livestock, 74
Llort, Fernando, 100, 105

M
man selling herbal remedies, *120*
mangrove forests, *28*, 31–33, *34*, *35*
manufacturing, 72, 74–75
maps
    colonial churches, *93*
    departments, *65*
    displaced peoples, *91*
    European exploration, *41*
    geographic, *16*
    geopolitical, *12*
    Pacific Ring of Fire, *18*
    population density, *86*
    resource, *74*
    San Salvador, 66
    United Provinces, *44*
maquiladoras, 75
Martí, Agustín Farabundo, 46–47
Martínez, Maximiliano Hernández, 46, *46*
massacre, 55
    at El Mozote, 53, 58
Mayan civilization, 9–10, 17–18, 37–38
    artifacts, 10
    calendar, 93
    ceramic bowl, *38*
    settlement, *37*
    stele replica, *36*

media, 124–126
Menéndez, César, 105
mestizos, 84–86
Metropolitan Cathedral, Interior, *92*
military
    coup, 51
    repression, 46–50
    rule, 47–50
    training, 54
mining, 72
Molina, Arturo Armando, 49, 81
money, 76, *76*
Morazán, Department of, 21
Morazán, Francisco, 21, *21*, 44
mountain ranges, 15, 20
mural art, *104*
Museum of Words and Images, 99
music, 103

N

National Civilian Police, 56, 60
National Palace, *62*
national parks and reserves, 35
    Bosque El Imposible, 30
    El Trifinio International Biosphere, 28
    Los Volcanes, 31
    Montecristo, 28–29, *29*
national symbols
    anthem, 67
    coat of arms, 63, *63*
    flag, 63, *63*
    izote flower, 27, *27*
    maquilishuat tree, 27
    motmot bird, 28, *28*
National Theater, 102, *102*
Nationalist Republican Alliance.
    See ARENA
natural resources, 21, 77–78
newspapers, 124–125
newsstand, *124*
Nueva San Salvador, 23

O

Operation Rescue, 53
Osorio, Oscar, 48

P

Pacific coast, 22, *22*, 24
painted toys, *100*
Pan American Highway, *79*
Panchimalco village, 83
panes con pavo (food), 123
Pangaea, 17
peace plan, 54
people
    elite landowners, 10, 13, 41, 43–44,
        45–46, 47–50, 52, 80–81
    emigration, 76
    employment, 71, 73, 75, 85–86, 87, 114
    family, 113–115
    famous, 133
    immigrants, 49, 76
    Indian decline, 83
    Mayan civilization, 9–10, 17–18, 37–38
    persecution and massacre, 47
    Pipil civilization, 38–39, 40
    population, 15, 27, 35, 91
    rebellion, 46–47
    refugees, 88–91
    Spanish colonists, 41–42
    Spanish conquerors, 40
    women, 86–88, 114
Perez, Francisco Flores, 61, *61*
Pipil civilization, 38–39, 40
plant life, 27–31
political discontent, 60–61
political parties, 67
pollution, 34, 121
Ponce, René Emilio, 58, *58*
poverty, 46–48, 85–86, 111–121
Protestant baptism, 96
Protestant community church, 97
pupusas (food), 123, *123*

R

radio, 126
ranching, 74
Reagan, Ronald, 52, 53
rebellion, 46–47, 49–50
Red Zone, 53
refugee family, 88
refugees, 88–91
religion
    Catholicism, 93–94
    diversity of El Salvador, 95
    Mayan, 93
    and the media, 96–97
    and politics, 94–96
    Protestant influence, 96–97
resources, 23
Río Lempa, 15, *15*, 24–25
rivers and lakes, 24–25
Rodriquez, Rafael Barraza, 63
Romero, Carlos Humberto, 51
Romero, Oscar, 50, *50*, 52, 58, 95
ruins of Mayan village, 9

S

Salarrué, 105
Salvadoran Communist Party, 46
Salvadoran family, *114*
Salvadoran protesters, *51*
SalvaNatura, 30–31, 35
San Miguel, 23
San Salvador, 66, *66*
Santa Ana, 23, *23*
school children, *116*
searching earthquake rubble, *14*
shantytown, *112*
shrimp farm workers, *73*
slavery, 41–42
soccer, 108–109
soccer game, *109*

Soccer War, 49
society
    class control, 10, 13, 41, 44, 45,
        47–50, 80–81, 85–86, 111–121
    colonial, 42
    role of women, 86–88, 114
Sol, Armando Calderón, 60, 70, *70*
sorpresas, 100–101
sports and leisure, 108–109

T

tamales (food), 123
Tamandua anteater, *30*
tankers at port, *80*
taxes, 42
Tazumal, 39, *39*
tectonic plates, 17
television, 125
textile workers, *75*
textiles, 101
trade
    colonial, 42
    early civilizations, 38, 39
    Spanish, 41
transportation, 46, 79–80
tree ducks, 32
Truth Commission, 57–59
TV station, *125*

U

United Nations, 56, 57, 60
United Provinces of Central America,
    43–44
United States
    accusation by Truth Commission, 58
    economic aid, 69
    land reform aid, 81
    support during civil war, 53, 55, 58
University of Central America entrance, *117*

V

Valenzuela, Rosa Mena, 104
village at base of volcano, 8
Volcano Illopango, 17–18
volcanoes, 9, 10, 13, 15, 17–20

W

water pollution, 34, 121
weights and measures, 81
wetlands, 31–35, 34
whistling ducks, 32
wildlife, 28–33, 35
woman
    carrying food basket, 82

making tortillas, *122*
of Palestinian descent, *84*
women
    cleaning coffee, *71*
    selling food, *85*
    training as soldiers, *87*
worker weaving textiles, *101*
workers storing sea salt, *77*
writers, 106–107

Z

Zaldivar, Rafael, 45
Zamora, Rubén, 59, 60

Meet the Author

I HAVE SPENT MOST OF MY ADULT LIFE TRAVELING IN LATIN America, studying and writing about the people and their way of life. In college, I earned a history degree, which has been enormously helpful for my research. Latin America has enjoyed a rich, varied, and often turbulent past. It has drawn me back time and time again. While writing this book, I often found myself remembering my early days when I was working with rural communities in the Andes Mountains. My life then touched the very simplest level of the dawn-to-dusk labor the Indians endured just to exist. I shall never forget many of the harsh experiences, but there always seemed to be hope in the air.

My research for this book began with the basic background. I then turned to the most up-to-date sources I could find, including people who had traveled to El Salvador recently. For me, the most difficult side of any book is separating the purely factual information from the more colorful and sometimes biased reports of visitors. I soon found that many people visited only San Salvador and went little farther than the tourist centers. Others, deeply attached to the country, have spent years in El Salvador, teaching in local communities, or helping with health or technical problems. The country is still trying to find its way after the long civil war. I shall remember the report of an old colleague who was the first reporter at the scene of the murder of Archbishop Romero. A day or so later, he visited the small town where the archbishop had been born. "It was a nice place," he wrote, "but everyone there including me was scared stiff of the police. I slept in the church as near to the altar as possible."

For general information, the Internet is a very useful tool, but one that needs to be used with caution. Often, I find that a telephone call in Spanish to the source quoted on the Web is better, as I can ask questions. One of the greatest joys of the Internet is access to daily newspapers in all countries, and every morning I read the local news from El Salvador and other places before I start work.

I continue to travel with my husband, Tony, who also writes books. Our two children are now starting their own careers. They return to Latin America whenever they can, and they also contribute to our library of pictures, which we have built up over many years.

Photo Credits